A GUIDE PORTUG_____ RAILWAYS

Caminhos de Ferro
Portugueses

David Clough Martin Beckett and Michael Hunt

First Edition

Published by: FEARLESS Publications, 23 Chestnut Drive, LEIGH, Lancs. WN7 3JW.

Printed by: BDC Printing Services Ltd., Slack Lane, Derby DE3 3FL.

© Fearless Publications and Milepost Publications 1991

INTRODUCTION

It is now quite some while since Platform 5 Publishing launched the first Continental spotters' book in the familiar format. Since then interest in Europe's railways has grown as the variety of motive power on BR has dwindled. Gradually more and more national fleets are being described and it will not be too long before Eastern European railways are added to the list.

What is surprising is that it has taken so long for a publisher to produce a book dealing with Portugal's national railways, the CP. Part of the reason is the small fleet size making the dedication of a monograph to the subject a difficult proposition. This book tackles the subject in a different way to previous spotters' books providing more than just number and allocation lists.

There is a brief description of the history of the CP and notes on how maintenance of traction and rolling stock is organised. This will assist visitors by pointing them to the places where the main works and depots can be found. The CP are normally happy to provide visitors with a permit for entry onto property and tight security prevails at the main installations, making the possession of such a permit essential (Address inside frontcover). Each class of locomotive is described thoroughly, with a most comprehensive table of dimensions, together with notes on salient features and the workings on which they could be found. In addition to the usual fleet and allocation lists, for the first time in a Continental book, track machines are included. All main line and most shunting locomotives and DMUs and EMUs are illustrated to assist initial identification.

It is hoped that this format will set a new standard for Continental railway books of the future. In connection with the production the authors acknowledge gratefully the assistance of the Chief PRO Dr. Américo Ramalho, and Eng. J.Simões of the CP, Gabinete de Informaciòn of RENFE (for 1321 technical data). Plus Geoff Hurst of Milepost Publications and Chris Appleby for the considerable material they have provided for this book. The railways of Portugal are varied and offer much interest which should delight the visitor who can observe over half of the CP fleet during a single week.

OUTLINE HISTORY

Railways were late in arriving and slow to develop in Portugal. The first section of line opened in 1856 between Lisbon (Lisboa), the capital, and Carregado, a distance of 37 km. This railway was extended over the next two decades in two directions. Elvas, on the Spanish frontier, was rail served in 1863, with Entroncamento, which became the junction for the two routes from Elvas and, later, Porto, being added to the map in 1864. Porto itself (the country's second city) had to wait until 1887 before final connection with the railway from Lisboa.

At the same time as these developments to the north of the River Tagus (Rio Tejo), the country to the south of the river was also being opened up. Barreiro, on the opposite bank of the river to Lisboa, and convenient ferry landing stage, was linked with Beja, a distance of 154 km. Construction continued throughout the latter part of the 19th century and into the 20th , with some links not being put in until the 1930s; the line to the large Atlantic port of Sines is a case in point. This slow pace of progress must, however, be seen in the context of the relatively small population, only around 10 million in 1989, with quite a wide dispersal outside the few large cities.

Track gauge followed Spanish practice and is 5ft 6ins (1.668 metres). Spanish practice was also followed in that some of the routes were constructed as metre gauge; this is found in the north. An advantage of the slow pace of development has been that few lines have closed, although some are now freight only. A major programme of closures took place on 1st January 1990, and the following lost their passenger service :-Valença - Monçao, Vila Real - Chaves, Sernada do Vouga - Viseu, Portalegre - Vila Viçosa, Évora - Estremoz, Beja - Moura and Ermidas Sado - Sines. Some lines became freight only. The route kilometres (miles) in 1987 was as follows:

	Broad Gauge		Metre Gauge	
	Single Track	Double Track	Single Track	Double Track
Electrified	54 (33¾)	404 (252½)		
Non-electrified	2,376(1485)	15 (9½)	752 (470)	6 (3¾)

This gives a total of 3,607km (2254½ miles). These figures reflect the intensity of the service, since the timetable for the non-electrified railways can be rather sparse, whilst that on the electrified sections can be very intensive.

Compania dos Caminhos de Ferro Portugueses became a joint stock company on 1st January 1947 with the amalgamation of all narrow gauge companies (Norte de Portugal, Companhia Nacional, and Val do Vouga) with the broad gauge Beira Alta Railway. Although part of the new grouping had been state owned prior to 1947, it was not until 1975 that the CP, as it is officially abbrievated, was nationalised. A noteable exception to these arrangements concerned the Estoril Railway. Although built by the Caminhos de Ferro Portugueses, starting in 1889, it was leased to Sociede Estoril for 50 years in 1926 and so did not come under public control until 1976.

The Estoril Railway is significant in another respect. This arises from it being the first route in Portugal to be electrified. The work was carried out as part of the lease and was to the then standard 1,500 volts dc system, using overhead power collection. It remained the only electrified line until 1957 and is still unique in that more recent electrified line until 1957 and is still unique in that more recent electrification (1957 and later) has been to the current standard of 25 kV 50 Hz AC.

NUMBERING SYSTEM

Following the amalgamation of companies on 1st January 1947 a new numbering scheme was adapted. Steam locomotives were numbered below 1000, with a 0 prefix for tank engines and an E prefix for narrow gauge steam, each forming seperate series. Diesel locomotives were given numbers in the 1xxx range, with 2xxx being applied to electric locomotives. Railcars and multiple units had a prefix letter system to denote gauge, corridor connections, motor or trailer, driving position and whether bogied.

From 1974 renumbering on the UIC system was adopted, bringing the use of 12 digits. Even so, locomotives continue to carry the old style four character number in addition to the new, longer version. The new numbers incorporate the old. Even post 1974 numbers fit into the old scheme. Non powered railcars, now numbered into the carriage series, also retain their old numbers. The new numbers are composed as follows:

Digits	1 & 2	Type and utilisation
	3 & 4	Denotes Portuguese ownership, so always 94
	5	Type of motive power - this is commonly the first digit actually carried on most stock (see below)
	6 & 7	UIC power rating in hundreds of horsepower; 00 for driving trailers and 99 for intermediate trailers
	8 - 11	Unit number; on metre gauge digit 8 is always 9
	12	Computer check number

Digit 5 denotes:

0	electric locomotive	5	diesel multiple unit trailer
1	diesel locomotive	6	diesel mechanical railcar/multiple unit
2	diesel shunter	7	diesel hydraulic railcar/multiple unit
3	steam locomotive	8	diesel electric railcar/multiple unit
4	not used	9	electric multiple unit

Railcar (ie non-mu) trailers, numbered in the new carriage series, use the digits 5 and 6 to denote seating layout and digits 7 and 8 are always 29. The actual numbers carried do not always correspond to the above system, since several instances of incorrect numbering have been observed.

The last digit of the UIC number is the computer check digit, this is used as a double check, to see whether all the preceding numbers are correct. The locomotive number is multiplied by 2 and 1. The resulting numbers are added together and then deducted from the next highest unit of ten will give the check digit.

Example – 90-94-1-101401

```
          9   0   9   4   1   1   0   1   4   0   1
      x   2   1   2   1   2   1   2   1   2   1   2

          1 + 8 + 1 + 8 + 4 + 2 + 1 + 0 + 1 + 8 + 0 + 2 =  36
```

40 - 36= 4

ORGANISATION OF ROLLING STOCK OVERHAUL, REPAIR and MAINTAINENCE

The way in which the CP organises this side of its business has been the subject of changes in the recent past and more changes are likely in the future. The following describes the postion during mid 1990.

Under the main board of directors a general director is responsible for all aspects of rolling stock maintainence. His command is divided as follows :

DMT - comprising the three main works.
DON - comprising the depots in the north.
DOS - comprising the depots in the south.
Sintra Line and Estoril Line.

DMT

This comprises the three main works or *grupo oficinas* (GOs), which are situated at Porto Custoias (1st GO), Entroncamento (2nd GO) and Barriero (3rd GO). Figueira da Foz used to be the 4th GO but was recently downgraded to the status of a maintainence shop. Its role as a depot will be dealt with later but it continues to overhaul Sentinel 1151 Class shunters and all broad gauge non stainless steel bodied coaches and the small fleet of sleeping cars.

The functions performed by the GOs are to overhaul, refurbish and rebuild locomotives and rolling stock and also to manufacture and overhaul components for use as spare parts at the depots. The work of each GO is as follows:

1st GO Custoias - the newest (opened 1990) works, responsible for overhaul of all metre gauge locomotives and rolling stock and DMUs in the 401 and 601 classes on the broad gauge.

2nd GO Entroncamento - overhaul of all AC electric locomotives and EMUs, all stainless steel coaches (90% of CP fleet), all broad gauge wagons, works repair of wheelsets, rewinding of all types of electrical machines (eg traction motors), manufacture of leaf springs and repair of all other types of springs, repairs to hydraulic dampers.

3rd GO Barreiro - overhaul of braod gauge diesel electric locomotives manufacture and repair of spare parts for diesel locomotives, overhauling and providing spares for CP ships.

DEPOT MAINTAINANCE

There are now five maintainence zones or divisions and these come under the control of one of the two Directions DON and DOS. In addition, the Sintra and Cintura Line andd the Estoril line have their own maintainence facilities.

DON (North Operations Direction):

This covers Zone 1 and is centred on Porto, comprising the following depots:

Campanhã - 401 and 601 Class DMUs, plus some coaches and wagons.
Contumil - 1401 Class diesels.
Boa Vista - All metre gauge rolling stock.

DOS (South Operations Direction):

This zone comprises the other four maintainence zones as follows:

Zone 2 Entroncamento - 2501 and 2551 Classes of electrics, 1151 Class shunters, 1401, 1551, and 1931 Classes of diesels, 2101 and 2151 Classes of EMUs, 20 coaches and 80% of CPs wagons, track machines.

Zone 3 Barriero - 1201, 1321, 1501, 1521, 1801 and 1901 Classes of diesels, 1101 Class of shunters and 101 Class railcars.

Zone 4 Figueira da Foz - comprising the two depots of Figueira da Foz and Coimbra B and the sub depot at Pampilhosa.
   Figueira da Foz - 1961 Class diesels, 651 Class DMUs;
   Coimbra B - 1401 Class diesels and 301 Class DMUs and coaches for the Beira-Alta line.

Zone 5 Lisboa - comprising the depots at Campolide and Santa Apolónia:
   Campolide - 2601 and 2621 Classes of electrics, 2001, 2051 and 2082 Classes of EMUs (Sintra and Cintura lines) and 2201 Class EMUs;
   Santa Apolónia - coaches (80% of CP fleet).

The depots in the above five zones carry out programmed maintenance and running repairs to the traction and rolling stock allocated in the same way that applies with a BR depot.

Estoril Line Direction

This is totally independent of the set up on the rest of the CP due to it only coming into the CP on nationalisation in 1976. It has a combined works and depot situated adjacent to its Lisboa Cais do Sodré station, though plans exist to relocate outside Lisboa.

In addition to the works and depots described above, fuelling, inspection and running repair facilities exist at a number of strategic locations on the CP. This is important for the metre gauge which comprises a number of isolated branches. These outposts on the metre gauge are at Livraçao, Régua, Mirandela and Sernada, whilst Boa Vista is adjacent to the first station out of Porto Trindade.

A computer based system is used to monitor and control traction and rolling stock maintenance. No such system is currently available for the running side dealing with the allocation of traction to services.

HOW TO GET THERE

By Rail: From London: Board any cross channel service from Victoria to Paris, and connect into the *"Sud Express"*. It leaves each morning from Paris (Austerlitz) taking just over 24 hours to Lisboa (Santa Apolónia), with a portion to Porto (Campanhã).

From Madrid: Two trains operate between Madrid (Chamartin) and Lisboa (Santa Apolónia). The day train is a TALGO *"Luis de Camões"* and takes just over 7 hours, the night service *"Lusitania Expresso"* takes about 12 hours.

By Air: Scheduled airlines (eg TAP/British Airways) operate from London Heathrow/Gatwick and Manchester to Lisboa, Porto and Faro. The cheapest way to fly is by charter flight only tickets to Faro (Algarve) and a limited service to Lisboa. Virtually all provincial airports have charter flights to Faro, you are advised to check brochures of Falcon, Horizon, Cosmos, Unijet Dan Air and others. Your travel agent will be able to find the best bargain.

ACCOMODATION

The authors are unable to recommend any accomodation, as they feel their choice may not suit every individual. We instead recommend you contact the Portuguese Tourist Offices listed below and they will supply various lists.

GREAT BRITAIN: Portuguese National Tourist Office, New Bond Street House, New Bond Street, LONDON W1Y 0NP. Tel. 071 493 3873

IRELAND: Portuguese Embassy (Tourist Information),Knocksinna House, Fox Rock, DUBLIN 18.Tel. 893569

Other Portuguese Tourist Offices can be found in Amsterdam, Brussel/Bruxelles, Frankfurt a. M., Paris, Madrid and Milano. All can be found in the telephone directory.

ALLOCATION CODES

The CP do not appear to use any allocation codes on there locomotives, however the date a locomotive left Barreiro Works is painted on the cabside proceded by the letters *BR*, presumably the code for the works. The following codes were created for this book.

Broad Gauge

BAR	Barreiro	CAS	Cais do Sodré	ENG	Engineers Department
CAP	Campolide (Lisboa)	COI	Coimbra B	ENT	Entroncamento
CAM	Campanhã (Porto)	CON	Contumil (Porto)	FIG	Figueira da Foz

Metre Gauge

BOA	Boa Vista (Porto)	MIR	Mirandela	SER	Sernada do Vouga
LIV	Livraçao	REG	Régua	Wdn	Withdrawn

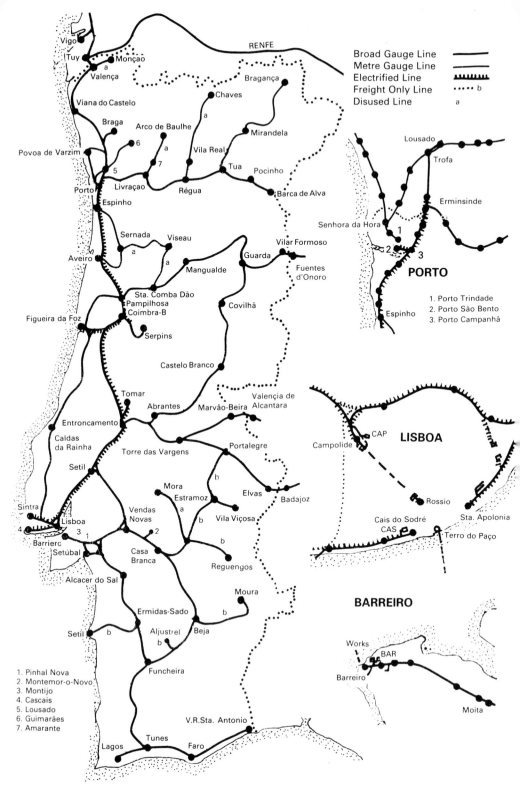

1. BROAD GAUGE DIESEL LOCOMOTIVES

1001–1006   C

Introduced 1948

BUILDERS

Mechanical Parts: The Drewry Car Co.
Diesel Engine: Gardner
Transmission: Self Changing Gears/Vulcan
Brakes: Westinghouse Brake & Signal Co.

Builder's Type Code: 0–6–0
Deadman's System: None
Speed Recorder: Drewry (indicator only)

DIMENSIONS

Height, overall: 3740 mm
Width: 2345 mm (over cab)
(Coupled) Wheelbase: 2740 mm

Height, over engine hood: 2890 mm
Length over buffers: 7815 mm
Wheel Diameter (new): 991 mm

PERFORMANCE

Maximum Speed: 41.5 km/h
Maximum Starting Tractive Effort: 7600 kg
Factor of Adhesion: (μ) 0.25
Tractive Effort at Maximum Speed: 1020 kg
Nominal Output at Rail: 150 CV

WEIGHTS

Weight in Working Order: 30.4 tonnes
Adhesive Weight: 30.4 tonnes
Maximum Axleload: 11 tonnes

SUPPLIES

Fuel Oil: 0.854 tonnes
Lubricating Oil: 0.045 tonnes
Coolant: 0.085 tonnes

DIESEL ENGINE

Number installed: 1
Builder: Gardner
Type: 8L3
Working Cycle: 4 stroke
Disposition & number of cylinders: 8 'in line'

Bore and Stroke: 137.7 x 196.9 mm
Speed (maximum): 1200 rpm
Piston–Swept Volume, total: 24 litres
Nominal Rating (to UIC 623): 200 CV
Site Rating: 200 CV

TRANSMISSION

Type: Mechanical
Fluid Coupling: (1) Vulcan–Sinclair
Gearbox: (1) Wilson–Drewry CA5
Final Drive: (1) SCG RF11
Final Transmission Ratio: 5.32:1

    These 0–6–0 shunting locomotives were constructed at Vulcan Foundry, Newton–le–Willows England, and are the eldest of the C.P.'s 'family' of British- built diesels, having given over forty years of sterling service. Readers familiar with the myriad of earlier British Rail diesel shunters will immediately recognise their close likeness to the Drewry Car Co.'s D2200 series (TOPS Class 04) - a type now long discarded on our national railway network although some are still in active in industrial service and in preservation. In fact, the C.P. '1001' class was a predecessor of our standard gauge variant. A visual difference is the absence on the C.P. locos of a cosmetic 'cone' around the engine final exhaust pipe. Other non- British features include the headlamp and the 'canopy' over the cab side windows.

    The Gardner engine delivers power, via a Vulcan–Sinclair fluid coupling, to a Wilson–Drewry type CA 5 five speed epicyclic gearbox, and then on to a Self Changing Gears type RF 11 spiral bevel reverse and final drive unit, complete with jackshaft.

Westinghouse straight air brakes are fitted to the locomotive and vacuum train braking equipment is provided.

The entire class is allocated to Contumil depot on the northern outskirts of Porto. They perform yard and station pilot duties in the general area. At Porto (Campanhã), they often share station pilot duties with the '1151' class 'Sentinels' and sometime even replace them, so that two can be found working there. One is often deployed as freight yard pilot at Contumil and another is outstationed at Régua on the Douro Valley route, where it performs shunting duties in the station yard.

UIC Number Series 90-94-2-01

	Depot	Notes		Depot	Notes		Depot	Notes
1001-9	CON		1003-5	CON		1005-0	CON	
1002-7	CON		1004-3	Wdn		1006-8	CON	

▲ Drewry 1001 Class shunter No.1002 propels the Porto portion of the "Sud Express" in Campanhã station on 1st May 1990. *(David N.Clough)*

▼ 1021 Class diesel shunter No.1025 is for departmental use only and are very rare to see. *(C.P.)*

1021–1025　　　　　　　　　　　　　　B

Introduced 1968

BUILDERS

Mechanical Parts: Gaston Moyse
Diesel Engine: Deutz
Transmission: Gaston Moyse
Brakes: Westinghouse

Builder's Type Code: BS 600 D
Deadman's System: None
Speed Recorder: 'HASLER'

DIMENSIONS

Height overall: 3810 mm
Width: 2980 mm
Length over buffers: 9090 mm

(Coupled) Wheelbase: 3700 mm
Wheel Diameter (new): 1050 mm

PERFORMANCE

Maximum Speed: 65 km/h
Maximum Starting Tractive Effort: 9720 kg
Tractive Effort at Continuous Rating: 9720 kg at 12 km/h
Tractive Effort at Maximum Speed: 1750 kg
Nominal Output at Rail: 425 CV

WEIGHTS

Weight, tare: 34.2 tonnes
Weight in Working Order: 36 tonnes
Adhesive Weight: 36 tonnes
Maximum Axleload: 18 tonnes

SUPPLIES

Fuel Oil: 0.751 tonnes
Lubricating Oil: 0.063 tonnes
Coolant: 0.18 tonnes
Sand: 0.63 tonnes

DIESEL ENGINE

Number installed: 1
Builder: Deutz
Type: BF 12M 716
Working Cycle: 4 stroke
Disposition & number of cylinders: V 12

Bore and Stroke: 135 x 160 mm
Speed (maximum): 1800 rpm
Piston–Swept Volume, total: 27.5 litres
Nominal Rating (to UIC 623): 625 CV
Site Rating: 625 CV

TRANSMISSION

Type: Electric
Maker: Gaston Moyse
Traction Generator: (2)
Traction Motors: (4)
Gear Ratio: 8.72:1

These smart looking Gaston Moyse machines are in fact rather obscure, since they usually function exclusively as departmental locomotives serving the Civil Engineer for the permanent way work and the like. Consequently, they can be seen on ballast trains and similar duties. They are equipped for train vacuum braking.

No.1024 was observed dumped at Figueira da Foz works during September 1986, having suffered fire damage. By April 1990 only the base of the frame survived.

UIC Number Series 90-94-2-04

	Depot	Notes		Depot	Notes		Depot	Notes
1021-1	ENG		1023-7	ENG		1025-2	ENG	
1022-9	ENG		1024-5	Wdn				

1051–1068 B

Introduced 1955

BUILDERS

Mechanical Parts: Gaston Moyse
Diesel Engine: Gaston Moyse
Transmission: Gaston Moyse
Brakes: Comp. des Freins Westinghouse

Builder's Type Code: BA
Deadman's System: Moyse
Speed Recorder: Moyse (indicator)

DIMENSIONS

Height, overall: 3775 mm
Height, over engine hood: 2930 mm
Width: 3120 mm

Length over buffers: 7280 mm
(Coupled) Wheelbase: 3128 mm
Wheel Diameter (new): 1050 mm

PERFORMANCE

Maximum Speed: 38 km/h
Maximum Starting Tractive Effort: 7000 kg
Factor of Adhesion: (μ) 0.25
Tractive Effort at Continuous Rating: 7000 kg at 4 km/h
Tractive Effort at Maximum Speed:
Nominal Output at Rail: 120 CV

WEIGHTS

Weight, tare: 27 tonnes
Weight in Working Order: 28.3 tonnes
Adhesive Weight: 28.3 tonnes
Maximum Axleload: 14.3 tonnes
Diesel Engine: 1.56 tonnes
Traction Motor: 2.15 tonnes

SUPPLIES

Fuel Oil: 0.835 tonnes
Lubricating Oil: 0.036 tonnes
Coolant: 0.114 tonnes
Sand: 0.15 tonnes

DIESEL ENGINE

Number installed: 1
Builder: Gaston Moyse
Type: M 6 A
Working Cycle: 4 stroke
Disposition & number of cylinders: 6 'in–line'

Bore and Stroke: 150 x 170 mm
Speed (maximum): 1500 rpm
Piston–Swept Volume, total: 18 litres
Nominal Rating (to UIC 623): 200 CV
Site Rating: 200 CV

TRANSMISSION

Type: Electric
Maker Gaston Moyse
Traction Generator d.c.: (1)
Traction Motors d.c.: (2)
Gear Ratio: 8.72:1

These unobtrusive, flexible little Gaston Moyse machines are particularly useful for light shunting duties. They perform general yard duties and the like, but have also been deployed as Barreiro Works pilot as well as at other engineering and industrial establishments.

Designed and built at the works of Établissements Gaston Moyse (Locotracteurs) outside of Paris, their general design and electric transmission have suffciently unusual features to justify further description.

The diesel engine features Ricardo combustion chambers. The engine and traction generator have rubber coupling between them. They are bolted separately to a deep channel section subframe which is elastically mounted on the locomotive frame structure. The engine is particularly over the centre of the wheelbase and the generator is sited over the leading axle.

The whole engine generator group is mounted to one side of the longitudinal centre line of the locomotive. This offset weight is balanced by that of the double armature traction motor which is offset to the other side and is located between the locomotive frames midway between the two axles. This offset of the motor gives room to the other side for the reduction gear connecting the two armatures to the output shaft and for the four sprockets which take the duplex chain drive to each axle. The force ventilated traction motor is wholly springborne, but is not suspended in conventional fashion, for it hangs on two large diameter through bolts going across from one main side frame plate to the other. Auxiliaries are belt and/ or cardan shaft driven.

Like the engines, the main generators and traction motors were built at the La Corneuve works of Gaston Moyse. This builder made nearly 100 per cent of the parts for this locomotive.

Only straight air and manual braking was originally installed and front and rear air sanding is fitted.

The derelict remains of No.1068 (May 1990) have been observed in the compound behind Barreiro fuel and inspection point, though little is intact above mainframe level.

UIC Number Series 90-94-2-01

	Depot	Notes		Depot	Notes		Depot	Notes
1051-4	ENT		1057-1	ENT		1063-9	Wdn	
1052-2	ENT		1058-9	Wdn		1064-7	ENT	
1053-0	BAR		1059-7	ENT		1065-4	BAR	
1054-8	ENT		1060-5	BAR		1066-2	Wdn	
1055-5	BAR		1061-3	Wdn		1067-0	Wdn	
1056-3	ENT		1062-1	ENT		1068-8	Wdn	1

1. Frame survives at Barreiro

▲ 1051 Class four wheel shunter No. 1059 in the Civil Engineer's depot at Entroncamento on 3rd May 1990. *(David N.Clough)*

1101–1112   Bo-Bo

Introduced 1949

BUILDERS

Mechanical Parts: General Electric
Diesel Engine: Caterpillar
Transmission: General Electric
Brakes: Westinghouse Air Brake

Builder's Type Code: B-B 90/90
Deadman's System: General Electric
Speed Recorder: RBM

DIMENSIONS

Height, overall: 3660 mm
Height, over engine hood:
Width: 2760 mm
Length over buffers: 10210 mm

Bogie Pivot Centres: 5630 mm
Bogie Wheelbase: 2085 mm
Wheel Diameter (new): 965 mm

PERFORMANCE

Maximum Speed: 56 km/h
Maximum Starting Tractive Effort: 10000 kg
Factor of Adhesion: (μ) 0.25
Tractive Effort at Continuous Rating: 4258 kg at 10 km/h
Tractive Effort at Maximum Speed: 1500 kg
Nominal Output at Rail: 255 CV

WEIGHTS

Weight, tare: 39 tonnes
Weight in Working Order: 41.2 tonnes
Adhesive Weight: 41.2 tonnes
Maximum Axleload: 10.3 tonnes
Traction Generator: 1.64 tonnes
Traction Motor: 1.13 tonnes
Bogies, complete: 2 x 7.1 tonnes

SUPPLIES

Fuel Oil: 0.793 tonnes
Lubricating Oil: 0.317 tonnes
Coolant: 0.38 tonnes
Sand: 0.544 tonnes

DIESEL ENGINE

Number installed: 2
Builder: Caterpillar
Type: D 17000
Working Cycle: 4 stroke
Disposition & number of cylinders: V 8

Bore and Stroke: 146 x 203 mm
Speed (maximum): 1000 rpm
Piston–Swept Volume, total: 27.3 litres
Nominal Rating (to UIC 623): 190 CV
Site Rating: 190 CV

TRANSMISSION

Type: Electric
Make: General Electric
Traction Generator (d.c.): (2) GT–555–A
Traction Motors (d.c.): (4) GE 733 (with reduction gearboxes)
Gear Ratio: 11.25:1

No one could mistake these distinctive, forty year old General Electric centre cab locomotives, designed in the U.S.A. by the General Electric Company of Schenectady, New York, and with diesel engines from the Caterpillar Tractor Company of Peoria, Illinois. In fact, they very closely resemble locomotives from the same builder which were supplied during 1945 for service on the Indian 5ft. 6in. gauge network, as well as units delivered for the North American domestic market.

Their original CP running numbers were D.E.1 - D.E.12, and they have several interesting features, not least of which is that they are twin engined , which is almost surprising if one considers their low combined power output. They are carried on Pennsylvania type bogies having plain bronze axlebox bearings. Worthy of inspection is the most interesting

12

and unusual arrangement by which each GE 733 traction motors drive its respective axle. Each cylindrical form self ventilated motor drives through double reduction spur gearing and is carried on the housing which encloses this gearing. The gear housing is axle mounted and spring supported from the bogie frame, Only vacuum train braking equipment is installed.

Most of the active survivors are allocated to Barreiro, and sometimes up to three can be seen in the station precincts at any given time, busily performing station and carriage siding pilot duties. Others are outstationed at such places as Barreiro freight terminal, Setúbal, and Vendas Novas.

UIC Number Series 90-94-2-02

	Depot	Notes		Depot	Notes		Depot	Notes
1101-5	BAR		1105-6	BAR		1109-8	FIG	
1102-3	FIG		1106-4	BAR		1110-6	BAR	
1103-1	BAR		1107-2	FIG		1111-4	BAR	
1104-9	BAR		1108-0	BAR		1112-2	Wdn	

▲ The 1101 Class shunters have two engines with a centre cab. Several can be found around Barreiro where they act as station and yard pilots. No.1111 stands outside Barreiro station in September 1989. (David N.Clough)

Introduced 1966–67

BUILDERS

Mechanical Parts: SOREFAME
Diesel Engine: Rolls Royce
Transmission: Rolls Royce/Alfred Wiseman
Brakes: Laycock Engineering

Builder's Type Code: 42t–SR
Deadman's System: Rolls Royce
Speed Recorder: Sentinel (indicator only)

DIMENSIONS

Height, overall: 3365 mm
Width: 2900 mm
Length over buffers: 8517 mm

Coupled Wheelbase: 2950 mm
Wheel Diameter (new): 1090 mm

PERFORMANCE

Maximum Speed: High Gear 58 km/h Low Gear 35 km/h
Maximum Starting Tractive Effort: High Gear 6600 kg
Factor of Adhesion: (μ)
Tractive Effort at Maximum Speed: High Gear 1000 kg Low Gear 1800 kg
Nominal Output at Rail: 250 CV

WEIGHTS

Weight, tare: 40.2 tonnes
Weight in Working Order: 42 tonnes
Adhesive Weight: 42 tonnes
Maximum Axleload: 14 tonnes
Diesel Engine: 1.54 tonnes
Hydraulic Transmission (Torque Converter): 0.61 tonnes
Final Drive: 1.334 tonnes

SUPPLIES

Fuel Oil: 1.18 tonnes
Lubricating Oil: 0.045 tonnes
Coolant: 0.085 tonnes
Sand: 0.27 tonnes

DIESEL ENGINE

Number installed: 1
Builder: Rolls Royce
Type: C8 TFL Mk 4
Working Cycle: 4 stroke
Disposition & number of cylinders: 8 'in line'

Bore and Stroke: 130.75 x 152.4 mm
Speed (maximum): 1800 rpm
Piston–Swept Volume, total: 16.2 litres
Nominal Rating (to UIC 623): 348 CV
Site Rating: 348 CV

TRANSMISSION

Type: Hydraulic
Torque Converter: Rolls Royce, Type CF 11 500
Final Drive: Alfred Wiseman, Type 15–DLGB/H
Gear Ratio: High Gear 6.33:1 (Low Gear 10.33:1)

Anyone enthusiastic about industrial locomotives should readily identify the Rolls–Royce/"Sentinel" body form. Interestingly, this Rolls–Royce product was the recipient of a Government sponsored "Council of Industrial Design" award on May 1st 1968. C.P. operates thirtysix of these useful machines, and the class is numerically the largest out of the five types of shunter. Clearly not bad for a railway administration which has decidedly *not* favoured diesel hydraulic traction!

They were constructed during 1966/67 by SOREFAME (Sociedades Reunidas de Fabricaçoes Metálicas S.A.R.L.) at Amadora, just six miles west of Lisboa, under a licence from Rolls–Royce/"Sentinel", Shrewsbury, England.

Equipment for train vacuum braking only is provided.

Their depot allocations reveal that the class is widespread; they can be seen at work at most major centres from Lisboa northwards, with a fair range of duties, including tripping.

UIC Number Series 90-94-2-02

	Depot	Notes		Depot	Notes		Depot	Notes
1151-0	ENT		1163-5	CAP		1175-9	COI	
1152-8	ENT		1164-3	CAP		1176-7	COI	
1153-6	ENT		1165-0	CAP		1177-5	COI	
1154-4	ENT		1166-8	CAP		1178-3	COI	
1155-1	ENT		1167-6	CAP		1179-1	COI	
1156-9	ENT		1168-4	CAP		1180-9	CON	
1157-7	ENT		1169-2	CAP		1181-7	CON	
1158-5	ENT		1170-0	CAP		1182-5	CON	
1159-3	CAP		1171-8	CAP		1183-3	CON	
1160-1	CAP		1172-6	CAP		1184-1	CON	
1161-9	CAP		1173-4	CAP		1185-8	CON	
1162-7	CAP		1174-2	COI		1186-6	CON	

▲ Familar Sentinel lines of 1151 Class. No. 1155 basks in the sun in a woodyard at Entroncamento during September 1989. *(David N.Clough)*

▼ Tunes is host to two 1201 Class locomotives No's 1221 and 1218, on 5th May 1990. They work the majority of Algarve Coast locals. *(David N.Clough)*

1201-1225

Bo-Bo

Introduced 1961–1964
Works No's Sorefame 1201-15 210-224/1216-25 334-343

BUILDERS

Mechanical Parts: SOREFAME
Diesel Engine: S.A.C.M.
Transmission: Brissonneau & Lotz
Speed Recorder: RBM 1201–1215 (indicator only), 'Hasler' 1216–1225

Brakes: Freins Jourdain–Monneret
Builder's Type Code: 040 DE
Deadman's System: Brissonneau & Lotz

DIMENSIONS

Height: 4030 mm
Width: 2800 mm
Length over buffers: 14680 mm

Bogie Pivot Centres: 7500 mm
Bogie Wheelbase: 2600 mm
Wheel Diameter (new): 1100 mm

PERFORMANCE

Maximum Speed: 80 km/h
Maximum Starting Tractive Effort: 16000 kg at **Factor of Adhesion:** (μ) 0.25
Tractive Effort at Continuous Rating: 12200 kg at 13 km/h
Tractive Effort at Maximum Speed: 1800 kg
Nominal Output at Rail: 600 CV

WEIGHTS

Weight, tare: 61.1 tonnes
Weight in Working Order: 64.7 tonnes
Adhesive Weight: 64.7 tonnes
Maximum Axleload: 16.5 tonnes
Diesel Engine: 4.3 tonnes
Traction Generator: 3.7 tonnes
Traction Motor: 2.3 tonnes
Bogies, complete: 2 x 14 tonnes

SUPPLIES

Fuel Oil: 2.5 tonnes
Lubricating Oil: 0.133 tonnes
Coolant: 0.365 tonnes
Sand: 0.45 tonnes

DIESEL ENGINE

Number installed: 1
Builder: S.A.C.M.
Type: MGO V 12 ASHR
Working Cycle: 4 stroke
Disposition & number of cylinders: V 12

Bore and Stroke: 175 x 180/192* mm
Speed (maximum): 1500 rpm
Piston–Swept Volume, total: 54 litres
Nominal Rating (to UIC 623): 825 CV
Site Rating: 825 CV

* MGO/AGO diesel engines have articulated connecting rods, resulting in a different piston stroke for each cylinder bank.

TRANSMISSION

Type: Electric (d.c.)
Traction Generator: (1) Brissonneau & Lotz B.L. 668–31
Traction Motors: (4) Brissonneau & Lotz 453–29
Gear Ratio: 69:16

These locomotives were constructed by SOREFAME at Amadora under a Brissonneau & Lotz licence. They are a standard low power line–service design by the latter company, which because of its acceptance by EUROFIMA (Société Européene por le Financement de Matérial Ferroviaire), can be found in France, Jugoslavia and Spain, as well as in Portugal. The means by which they were acquired by the CP is of interest, for these were the first line–service locomotives of European type and build to operate on the CP system. The first contract was for nine units ordered through and financed EUROFIMA. At the same time another six were ordered direct by the CP from Brissonneau & Lotz, with construction of both orders to be by SOREFAME and Brissonneau & Lotz in collaboration.

The first to be completed, left SOREFAME works in February 1961 and was presented officially at Lisboa's (Santa Apolónia) terminus on March 7th. The final ten locomotives constituted a later repeat order.

A feature of interest in these and in other CP locomotives, is the MGO vee—form engine. All manufacturing and marketing rights to which are held by the Société Alsacienne de Constructions Méchaniques de Mulhouse (S.A.C.M.). The letters M.G.O represent Mariep—Grosshans—Ollier, the middle word being the name of the designer, and the two end words being the names of those who provided the financial and commercial facilities. However, since the mid 1960's the Grosshans engine has been marketed by S.A.C.M. as the 'AGO' in response to a change in sponsorship, and other factors.

A noteworthy feature is its articulated connecting rod arrangement, though this is by no means unique to this design of engine. Each piston contained in one bank of cylinders drives directly onto its respective crankpin through a 'master' connecting rod. The connecting rods of opposite pistons in the other cylinder bank, drive not onto the relevant crankpins as usually is the case, but onto an 'articulation' joint borne by a boss on the enlarged big end of each 'master' connecting rod. This curious arrangement produces a different piston stroke (and piston speed) for each cylinder bank, the pistons driving the 'articulated' connecting rods having longer strokes than those driving the 'master' rods.

These characteristically French locomotives are equipped only for vacuum train braking, and have no multiple—unit facility. 'Lubrovia' wheelflange lubricators are fitted as standard.

The Campolide (Lisboa) locomotives (on the line out of Rossio terminus) undertake local trip workings onto the Lisboa - Porto mainline, a typical destination being the cement works at Alhandra. The remainder operate from Barreiro and perform light passenger and freight duties all over the Southern Region, including some Barreiro-Setúbal commuter locals. They also work locals to Beja and the branch service from Casa Branca to Évora. Virtually all the Algarve coastal services between Lagos, Tunes, Faro and Vila Real Sto.—Antonio—Guadiana near the Spanish frontier.

UIC Number Series 90-94-1-06

	Depot	Notes		Depot	Notes		Depot	Notes
1201-6	CAP		1210-7	BAR		1219-8	BAR	
1202-4	CAP		1211-5	BAR		1220-6	BAR	
1203-2	CAP		1212-3	BAR		1221-4	BAR	
1204-0	CAP		1213-1	BAR		1222-2	BAR	
1205-7	BAR		1214-9	BAR		1223-0	BAR	
1206-5	BAR		1215-6	BAR		1224-8	BAR	
1207-3	BAR		1216-4	BAR		1225-5	BAR	
1208-1	BAR		1217-2	BAR				
1209-9	BAR		1218-0	BAR				

TIMETABLE

The CP produce two 'Guia Horario Oficial' (timetables) - Summer *Veráo* and Winter *Inverno*. They can be purchased in the UK from B.A.S Overseas Publications Ltd.,Unit 1C, 159 Mortlake Road, KEW, Surrey TW9 4AW. or from any CP station at about 200$00.

1301–1312   A1A-A1A

During 1952 the CP took delivery of twelve A1A–A1A centre cab diesel electric locomotives from the Whitcomb Locomotive Company of Rochelle, Illinois, U.S.A. (a subsidiary of the Baldwin–Lima–Hamilton Corporation). They were of Whitcomb type 104DE2 classification and bore serial numbers 61156 – 61167 in sequence. Each hood contained a Superior 660 hp six cylinder in–line diesel engine together with its associated generators etc., thus these were twin power unit locomotives. Electrical equipment was supplied by the American Westinghouse Co.

In their early years they were deployed working both freight and passenger services north of the Rio Tejo (River Tagus). Although they seem to have ended their days based at Barreiro, where they undertook local trip work, and even appeared on the Algarve Coastal line on passenger duties. The first withdrawals commenced in the early 1980's, although 1311 received an overhaul at Barreiro Works as late as July 1983. It is understood that 1303 and 1308 were scrapped by 1985, but 1302/04/06 were still in service in September 1986. All were out of service by February 1987.

UIC Number Series 90-94-1-10

	Depot	Notes		Depot	Notes		Depot	Notes
1301-6	Wdn	1	1305-7	Wdn	2	1309-9	Wdn	
1302-4	Wdn		1306-5	Wdn		1310-7	Wdn	2
1303-2	Wdn		1307-3	Wdn	1	1311-5	Wdn	1
1304-0	Wdn		1308-1	Wdn		1312-3	Wdn	

1. Dumped in yard at Barreiro
2. Dumped behind Barreiro roundhouse

▲ Whitcomb No.1301 departs from Tunes with the Lagos portion of the 0850 from Barreiro on 13th July 1983. *(P.G.Barnes)*

1321–1338   Co-Co

Introduced 1965 (RENFE Class 313)/ 1989 onwards (CP)

BUILDERS

Mechanical Parts: 313.001–040 Compañia Euskalduna 313.041–050 ALCO
Diesel Engine: ALCO
Transmission: GENERAL ELECTRICA (Español)/GENERAL ELECTRIC
Brakes: WABCO-DIMETAL (originally air on locomotive, vacuum on train)·
Builder's Type Code: DL 535 T & S
Deadman's System: Yes
Licence: ALCO PRODUCTS INC.

DIMENSIONS

Height: 4032 mm
Width: 2864 mm
Bogie Pivot Centres: 10465 mm

Wheel Diameter (new): 1016 mm
Length over buffers: 16237 mm
Bogie Wheelbase: 3505 mm(1676 mm+1829 mm)

PERFORMANCE

Maximum Speed: 120 km/h
Maximum Starting Tractive Effort (limit of adhesion): 18480kg & **Factor of Adhesion** (μ) : 0.22
Tractor Effort at Continuous Rating: 19300 at 14 km/h (unable to utilized for adhesive reasons)
Effective Value: 13743 kg at 20 km/h
Tractive Effort at Maximum Speed: 1850 kg
Nominal Output at Rail: 1010 CV (743kW)

WEIGHTS

Weight, tare: 77.4 tonnes
Weight in Working Order: 83.9 tonnes (full provisions)
Weight in Working Order: 81.7 tonnes (²⁄₃ provisions)
Adhesive Weight: 83.9 tonnes (full provisions)
Adhesive Weight: 81.7 tonnes (²⁄₃ provisions)
Maximum Axleload: 13.987 tonnes
Diesel Engine: 10.8 tonnes
Traction Generator (with auxilary): 5.3 tonnes
Traction Motor: 1.66 tonnes
Bogies, complete: 2 x 15.4 tonnes

SUPPLIES

Fuel Oil: 2.17 tonnes
Lubricating Oil: 0.48 tonnes
Coolant: 0.54 tonnes
Sand: 0.51 tonnes
Boiler Water (locos as built): 2.65 tonnes

DIESEL ENGINE

Number installed: 1
Builder: ALCO PRODUCTS INC.
Type: 6-251-D
Working Cycle: 4 stroke
Disposition & number of cylinders: 6, in line
Bore and Stroke: 228.6 x 266.7 mm

Speed (maximum): 1100 r.p.m
Piston–Swept Volume, total: 65.7 tonnes
Turbocharged: Yes
Nominal Rating (to UIC 623): 1370 CV
Site Rating: 1370 CV

TRANSMISSION

Traction Generator: (1) General Electric Type GT - 581 E
Traction Motors: (6) General Electric Type 5 GE - 761
Gear Ratio: 92:19

RHEOSTATIC BRAKE

Maximum Braking Effort: 14060 kg at 30 km/h

At the time of going to press, information about these locomotives is somewhat limited, since they only appeared on the C.P. network during the latter half of 1989. At least twelve maybe eighteen have been purchased second hand from R.E.N.F.E. (Spanish National Railways) where they have become surplus to requirements. They were first introduced during 1965 and belonged to R.E.N.F.E.'s '313' class, of which fifty were originally constructed. No.s 1301-40 came from Compañia Euskalduna at Bilbao and no.s 1341-50 from ALCO at Schenectady (serial nos 3417-01 to 10 of 1965). During their latter years in Spain, the entire class operated from Granada depot.

Following purchase, each unit is being overhauled by Ateinsa Aplicaciones Tecnicas Industriales S.A. in their works near the station at Villaverde Bajo in Madrid. The first few so tested are being deployed, for the present at least, at Barriero and are confined to freight duties. They work the cement traffic from Sines to Alhandra Cement Works on the Lisboa to Entroncamento route. During early 1990, one stabled in the Cement works yard, and was visible from the line.

They are an ALCO single—cab design, quite North American in general appearance, with the cab sandwiched between a long and short hood. A dual train braking is installed. The ALCO diesel engine has a six cylinder in— line configuration. A dual braking system is installed.

Nos. 1321 and 1322 are ex RENFE 313.011 and 313.039, however the order of renumbering is at present unknown.

UIC Number Series 90-94-1-10

	Depot	Ex RENFE		Depot	Ex RENFE		Depot	Ex RENFE
1321-4	BAR	313	1327-1	BAR	313	1333-9		313
1322-2	BAR	313	1328-9	BAR	313	1334-7		313
1323-0	BAR	313	1329-7	BAR	313	1335-4		313
1324-8	BAR	313	1330-5	BAR	313	1336-2		313
1325-5	BAR	313	1331-3	BAR	313	1337-0		313
1326-3	BAR	313	1332-1		313	1338-8		313

▲ 1321 Class No. 1321 stands on the turntable at Barreiro in September 1989. The logo and numbers are non CP standard. *(David N.Clough)*

1401-1467　　　　　　　　　　　　　　　Bo-Bo

Introduced 1966–69
Works No's: 1401-10 EE 3758-67/Vulcan Foundry D1127-36
　　　　　　　1411-50 SOREFAME 498-537/628-44

BUILDERS

Mechanical Parts: 1401-10 English Electric Co. 1411-67 SOREFAME
Diesel Engine: English Electric Co.　　　**Transmission:** English Electric Co.
Brakes: Westinghouse Brake & Signal Co.　**Builder's Type Code:** LD 844 C
Deadman's System: Davies & Metcalfe/Oerlikon　**Speed Recorder:** 'HASLER'

DIMENSIONS

Height (over cab roof): 4355 mm　　　**Bogie Pivot Centres:** 6550 mm
Width: 3260 mm　　　　　　　　　**Bogie Wheelbase:** 2360 mm
Length over buffers: 12720 mm　　　**Wheel Diameter (new):** 950 mm

TRANSMISSION

Type: Electric (d.c.)
Traction Generator: (1) English Electric Co. EE 819/9H
Traction Motors: (4) English Electric Co. EE 548/3A
Gear Ratio: 72:15

PERFORMANCE

Maximum Speed: 105 km/h
Maximum Starting Tractive Effort: 16100 kg at **Factor of Adhesion:** (μ) 0.25
Tractive Effort at Continuous Rating: 14200 kg at 19 km/h
Tractive Effort at Maximum Speed: 2400 kg
Nominal Output at Rail: 970 CV

WEIGHTS

Weight, tare: 60.8 tonnes
Weight in Working Order: 64.4 tonnes
Adhesive Weight: 64.4 tonnes
Maximum Axleload: 16.3 tonnes
Diesel Engine: 12.09 tonnes
Traction Generator: 4.76 tonnes
Traction Motor: 2.04 tonnes
Bogies, complete: 2 x 11.2 tonnes

SUPPLIES

Fuel Oil: 1.878 tonnes
Lubricating Oil: 0.38 tonnes
Coolant: 0.47 tonnes
Sand: 0.66 tonnes

DIESEL ENGINE

Number installed: 1
Builder: English Electric Co.
Type: 8 CSVT (Mk2)
Working Cycle: 4 stroke
Disposition & number of cylinders: V 8
Bore and Stroke: 254.0 x 304.8 mm
Speed (maximum): 850 rpm
Piston—Swept Volume, total: 123.5 litres
Nominal Rating (to UIC 623): 1370 CV
Site Rating: 1328 CV
Turbocharged: Yes

　　These delightful 'steeple' cab machines represented a significant breakthrough in the export field for English Electric's Traction Division, since they were the first mainline locomotives ordered for mainland Europe - and against fierce competition from European industry. Only sundry shunting locomotives had been supplied to the Continent prior to this order.

　　The first ten locomotives were constructed at Vulcan Works on Merseyside. The order (EE contract CCT 1401) was dated November 10th 1965. It included an arrangement for a further forty, C.P. Nos. 1411–1450. which were built in Portugal under licence by SOREFAME at Amadora (just outside Lisboa) using major traction components shipped from England. A further seventeen (Nos. 1451–1467) were ordered later, at the same time as the '1801' class, and were also constructed under licence by SOREFAME.

The diesel engine may be loosely regarded as 'half a B.R. Class 50 Engine', but using a pair of Napier HP100SA turbochargers. The traction generator is a version of that installed in British Rail's Class 20. The EE548 traction motors are basically a design for metre gauge locomotives. All auxiliaries, with the exception of the two vacuum exhausters, have mechanical rather than electric drives.

On account of the special interest which attaches to these British designed locomotives, some particulars of the English Electric traction equipment are summarized below.

Diesel Engine - This is of model 8CSVT Mk.II. The reduced site rating of these machines is a direct consequence of conditions encountered in Portugal, where sea level ambient temperatures in the south can reach 40°C, and maximum route altitude is 900 m (2,700 ft) in the north. In , total, seventy two engines were supplied to Portugal for the sixty seven locomotives. These carry the following serial numbers -

IH 6390 (Prototype) Total 1
IH 6815 - 6834
IH 6859 - 6890 Total 52
IH 7357 - 7375 Total 19

Continuous full field ratings for the principal electrical machines are as follows -
Traction Generator - EE819/9H, six pole. 850 kW, 1220 A, 700 V at 850 rpm.
Auxiliary Generator - EE736/7K, four pole, belt driven. 19.8 kW, 180 A, 110 V over speed range 1200 - 2270 rpm.
Traction Motor - EE548/3A, four pole. 242 hp, 600 A, 350 V at 477 rpm.

Equipment for dual (air/vacuum) train braking is installed on twenty three examples of the class, selected at random. The remainder having provision for train vacuum braking only. 'Lubrovia' wheel flange lubricators are standard. These locomotives can operate in multiple only with themselves and the EE '1801'class, up to a total of three units.

Numerically this is the largest diesel class on the CP. Five have been written off to date, including No. 1439 which was destroyed, together with Bombardier diesel No. 1961 in a horrific head on collision and fire on the Beira Alta line involving the Sud Express.

Operationally, their allocation is divided between three depots, but they can be found virtually all over the CP network. Those based at Porto (Contumil) cover the loco hauled services from Porto's São Bento terminus, both along the Douro Valley line to Marco de Canaveses, Régua, and Pocinho and also northwards to Valença do Minho. They also cover freight duties on these routes and are thus the only mainline broad gauge diesels found north of Contumil. Coimbra B's fleet works secondary passenger trains along the Beira Alta line from Vilar Formoso to Pampilhosa and Coimbra, together with some passenger turns from Alfarelos to Caldas do Rainha and Lisboa's Rossio terminus. They can also be seen hauling freight on these and associated lines. Entroncamento turns out its allocation on secondary passenger services from that point eastwards to Badajoz in España (latest information is that although advertised as a through service the locomotive hauled passenger trains terminate at Portalegre, with a dmu forward). However this depots' allocation is deployed mainly on freight work, both east and west of Entroncamento, whilst at least a few find deployment south of the Rio Tejo (River Tagus) on freight workings down to the Algarve coast or on local secondary passenger duties out of Barreiro terminus. Since they visit Barreiro Works for overhaul, they can often be observed in ex works condition on running in turns to Pinhal Novo.

UIC Number Series 90-94-1-10

	Depot	Notes		Depot	Notes		Depot	Notes
1401-4	CON		1424-6	CON		1447-7	COI	
1402-2	CON		1425-3	CON		1448-5	COI	
1403-0	Wdn		1426-1	CON		1449-3	COI	
1404-8	CON		1427-9	CON		1450-1	COI	
1405-5	CON		1428-7	CON		1451-9	COI	
1406-3	CON		1429-5	CON		1452-7	COI	
1407-1	CON		1430-3	CON		1453-5	COI	
1408-9	CON		1431-1	CON		1454-3	COI	
1409-7	CON		1432-9	CON		1455-0	COI	
1410-5	CON		1433-7	Wdn		1456-8	ENT	
1411-3	CON		1434-5	CON		1457-6	ENT	
1412-1	CON		1435-2	CON		1458-4	ENT	
1413-9	CON		1436-0	COI		1459-2	ENT	
1414-7	CON		1437-8	COI		1460-0	ENT	
1415-4	CON		1438-6	COI		1461-8	ENT	
1416-2	CON		1439-4	Wdn		1462-6	ENT	
1417-0	CON		1440-2	COI		1463-4	ENT	
1418-8	CON		1441-0	CON		1464-2	ENT	
1419-6	CON		1442-8	COI		1465-9	CON	
1420-4	Wdn		1443-6	Wdn		1466-7	CON	
1421-2	CON		1444-4	COI		1467-5	CON	
1422-0	CON		1445-1	COI				
1423-8	CON		1446-9	COI				

▲ One of Entroncamento's 1401 Class finds its way to the Algarve on coal hoppers for Loule. No.1461 shunts at Tunes in September 1989. *(David N.Clough)*

1501–1512/1521–1525*   A1A–A1A

Introduced 1948/1951* (All uprated at Barreiro from 1500 hp to 2000 hp throughout the 1970's)
Works No.s: 75872-75883/79069*/71*/4*/7*/80*

BUILDERS

Mechanical Parts: ALCO
Diesel Engine: ALCO
Transmission: GENERAL ELECTRIC
Brakes: Knorr–Bremse

Builder's Type Code: RSC 3
Deadman's System: None is fitted
Speed Recorder: 'HASLER'

DIMENSIONS

Height: 4385 mm
Width: 3025 mm
Bogie Pivot Centres: 9143 mm
Wheel Diameter (new): 1016 mm

Length over buffers: 16988 mm
Bogie Wheelbase: 3352 mm

PERFORMANCE

Maximum Speed: 120 km/h
Maximum Starting Tractive Effort: 17000 kg (17200 kg*) at **Factor of Adhesion:** (μ) 0.22
Tractive Effort at Continuous Rating: 21000 kg at 21 km/h (unable to be utilized for adhesive weight reasons.)
Tractive Effort at Maximum Speed: 3800 kg
Nominal Output at Rail: 1730 CV

WEIGHTS

Weight, tare: 105 (108*) tonnes
Weight in Working Order: 111 (114*) tonnes
Adhesive Weight: 76 (78*) tonnes
Maximum Axleload: 19 (19.5*) tonnes
Diesel Engine: 14.62 tonnes
Traction Generator: 4.74 tonnes
Traction Motor: 3.28 tonnes
Bogies, complete: 2 x 21.1 tonnes

SUPPLIES

Fuel Oil: 2.53 tonnes
Lubricating Oil: 0.89 tonnes
Coolant: 0.95 tonnes
Sand: 1.2 tonnes

DIESEL ENGINE

Number installed: 1
Builder: ALCO
Type: 251–C
Working Cycle: 4 stroke
Disposition & number of cylinders: V 12
Bore and Stroke: 228.6 x 266.7 mm

Speed (maximum): 1025 rpm
Piston–Swept Volume, total: 131.4 litres
Nominal Rating (to UIC 623): 2185 CV
Site Rating: 2185 CV
Turbocharged: Yes

TRANSMISSION

Type: Electric (d.c.)
Traction Generator: (1) General Electric 5 GT 564–B1 (5 GT 564–C1*)
Traction Motors: (4) General Electric 5 GE 752–A1
Gear Ratio: 65:18

These are the CP's oldest mainline diesel locomotives. The original delivery of twelve units (current CP running numbers 1501–1512) arrived in 1948 almost coincidentally with the arrival of the Drewry shunters of Class 1001. The original CP running numbers applied to these twelve locomotives were arranged to divide the batch into two series, Nos. DE.101-106 and DE.1101–1106. This curious scheme did not reflect any detail differences or the like. It was merely a relic of an earlier CP numbering system which segregated locomotives within any given class according to geographical region of allocation.

As originally delivered these machines had an ALCO Series 244 12 cylinder diesel engine in 'vee' formation, with 9 inch by 10½ inch (229 mm x 267 mm) cylinders and of 1650 bhp gross output, giving a traction input to the main generator of 1520 bhp at 1000 rpm. In this condition, the manufactures type code was RSC 2. The 1951 series was delivered as nos DE 121-125, and was marginally more powerful, being of model RSC 3u and of a nominal 1600 hp traction input to the main generator.

Both these and the later series delivered in 1951 were given a new lease of life during the 1970's when they were uprated at Barreiro Works, by the installation of ALCO 251-C diesel engines supplied by MLW. The ALCO Series 251 range of oil engines was originally introduced, in in-line form, during the first half of 1953, and the first vee-form engine was installed in a locomotive in the beginning of 1954. It has proven to be much more robust and trouble free design than its predecessors.

Being typical North American 'road switchers' of their period, the only real visual 'give away' that they are an export version of U.S. home market models is the provision of side buffing gear. They even sport the all round outer handrails and stanchions so beloved of American practice, and their builder's plates proudly proclaim that they were manufactured at Schenectady, N.Y., U.S.A.

Both batches of locomotives are carried on bogies of the Pennsylvania type with compensatory beams between the tops of the roller bearing axleboxes and supported by helical steel springs. Nowadays they are equipped with an air/vacuum dual train braking system, but have no facility for multiple unit operation. FIAT wheel flange lubricators are fitted as standard.

When new they were deployed on a variety of passenger and freight duties between Lisboa and Porto and onto the Spanish frontier. Nowadays, being entirely based at Barreiro, and they operate exclusively on the Southern Region. They perform sterling work on the Barreiro – Setúbal commuter trains, as well as some duties to Beja and Funcheira. They can even deputise for 1801 or 1901 class locomotives on Barreiro – Algarve 'Inter Regionals' and other services. Freight activity occupies approximately half of their duties and they traverse much of the routes in the region, either singly or in tandem with a smaller diesel on heavier duties.

UIC Number 90-94-1-17

	Depot	Rebuilt		Depot	Rebuilt		Depot	Rebuilt
1501-6	BAR	09.73	1505-7	BAR	04.76	1509-9	BAR	02.71
1502-4	BAR	02.74	1506-5	BAR	01.77	1510-7	BAR	01.71
1503-2	BAR	08.74	1507-3	BAR	02.73	1511-5	BAR	05.74
1504-0	BAR	06.73	1508-1	BAR	01.73	1512-3	BAR	05.74

UIC Number 90-94-1-17

	Depot	Rebuilt		Depot	Rebuilt		Depot	Rebuilt
1521-4	BAR	07.75	1523-0	BAR	06.78	1525-5	BAR	12.73
1522-2	BAR	12.74	1524-8	BAR	12.75			

▲ Typical North American road switcher design, represented by the 1501 and 1521 Classes. No. 1501 waits its next duty at Barreiro in September 1989. *(David N.Clough)*

▼ 1551 Class are typical North American road switcher design. They differ from the 1501 and 1521 Classses by having a different cab and body design which is angular. No.1567 stands beneath Entroncamento depots watertower during September 1989. *(David N.Clough)*

1551–1570

Introduced 1973
Works No. M6066–01-20

BUILDERS

Mechanical Parts: MLW
Diesel Engine: MLW/ALCO
Transmission: Canadian General Electric
Brakes: WABCO

Builder's Type Code: MX–620
Deadman's System: Davies & Metcalfe
Speed Recorder: 'HASLER'

DIMENSIONS

Height: 4356 mm
Width: 2997 mm
Wheel Diameter (new): 1016 mm

Bogie Wheelbase: 3403 mm
Length over buffers: 17905 mm

PERFORMANCE

Maximum Speed: 120 km/h
Maximum Starting Tractive Effort: 24300 kg at **Factor of Adhesion:** (μ) 0.27
Tractive Effort at Continuous Rating: 19300 kg at 22.5 km/h
Tractive Effort at Maximum Speed: 4000 kg
Nominal Output at Rail: 1700 CV

WEIGHTS

Weight, tare: 83.4 tonnes
Weight in Working Order: 89.7 tonnes
Adhesive Weight: 89.7 tonnes
Maximum Axleload: 15.4 tonnes
Diesel Engine: 14.63 tonnes
Traction Generator: 5.50 tonnes
Traction Motor: 1.89 tonnes
Bogies, complete: 2 x 16.7 tonnes

SUPPLIES

Fuel Oil: 3.34 tonnes
Lubricating Oil: 0.888 tonnes
Coolant: 1.319 tonnes
Sand: 0.6 tonnes

DIESEL ENGINE

Number installed: 1
Builder: MLW/ALCO
Type: 251–C3
Working Cycle: 4 stroke
Disposition & number of cylinders: V 12
Bore and Stroke: 228.6 x 266.7 mm

Speed (maximum): 1050 rpm
Piston–Swept Volume, total: 131.4 litres
Nominal Rating (to UIC 623): 2180 CV
Site Rating: 2180 CV
Turbocharged: Yes

TRANSMISSION

Type Electric (d.c.)
Traction Generator: (1) Can. General Electric 5 GT 851–Pj1
Traction Motors: (6) Can. General Electric 5 GE 761
Gear Ratio: 92:19

In 1948, the Montreal Locomotive Works Ltd. (MLW) became an ALCO-GE diesel electric locomotive builder Licensee. The controlling American Locomotive Company (since 1956 renamed ALCO Products, Inc.) ceased locomotive production at Schenectady in January 1969, and, later that year, ALCO Products Inc. sold the locomotive designs outright to MLW, excluding the design rights to the diesel engine. MLW was operated by MLW-Worthington until 1975.

The '1551' class (constructed under MLW Sales Order No. 4721) is a typical MLW product, and one which is also very typical of North American 'hood unit' practice in general. They are an export version of types operating in large numbers on Canadian railways. As with the 1501/1521 series of ALCO built units, the visual 'give away' of their export nature is the presence of side buffers. With the MLW class there is also an absence of outside handrails and stanchions along the full length of the 'long hood'.

They are equipped with an air/vacuum dual train braking system, and can operate in multiple with themselves, up to a total of two units.

The entire class is based at Entroncamento depot. They work passenger trains from Entroncamento to Covilhã and Guarda, as well as 'Rapidos' and locals on the Beira – Alta line from Pampilhosa to Vilar Formoso on the Spanish Border. They work freight trains in Eastern Portugal and are regularly used on 'Inter Regional' freights onto the Southern Region to the docks at Setúbal via Setil.

UIC Number 94-90-1-21

	Depot Notes		Depot Notes		Depot Notes
1551-3	ENT	1558-8	ENT	1565-3	ENT
1552-1	ENT	1559-6	ENT	1566-1	ENT
1553-9	ENT	1560-4	ENT	1567-9	ENT
1554-7	ENT	1561-2	ENT	1568-7	ENT
1555-4	ENT	1562-0	ENT	1569-5	ENT
1556-2	ENT	1563-8	ENT	1570-3	ENT
1557-0	ENT	1564-6	ENT		

▲ 1808 on the (9010) 0810 V.R.Sto António-Guardiana to Barreiro train passes Álcacer do Sal on 16th March 1988. (David N.Clough)

1801–1810   Co-Co

Introduced 1969
Works No.s EE 3882-91/Vulcan Foundry D1246-55

BUILDERS

Mechanical Parts: English Electric Co.
Diesel Engine: English Electric Co.
Transmission: English Electric Co.
Deadman's System: Davies & Metcalfe/Oerlikon
Speed Recorder: 'HASLER'

Brakes: Westinghouse Brake & Signal Co.
Builder's Type Code: LD 937 B

DIMENSIONS

Height: 4265 mm
Width: 3260 mm
Bogie Pivot Centres: 10494 mm
Wheel Diameter (new): 1100 mm

Length over buffers: 18680 mm
Bogie Wheelbase: 4114 mm

PERFORMANCE

Maximum Speed: 140 km/h
Maximum Starting Tractive Effort: 26000 kg
Tractive Effort at Continuous Rating: 17750 kg at 31 km/h
Tractive Effort at Maximum Speed: 3300 kg
Nominal Output at Rail: 2020 CV

WEIGHTS

Weight, tare: 103.6 tonnes
Weight in Working Order: 110.3 tonnes
Adhesive Weight: 110.3 tonnes
Maximum Axleload: 18.8 tonnes
Diesel Engine: 20.85 tonnes
Traction Generator: 6.40 tonnes
Traction Motor: 2.72 tonnes
Bogies, complete: 2 x 22 tonnes

SUPPLIES

Fuel Oil: 3.795 tonnes
Lubricating Oil: 0.552 tonnes
Coolant: 1.36 tonnes
Sand: 0.8 tonnes

DIESEL ENGINE

Number installed: 1
Builder: English Electric Co.
Type: 16 CSVT (Mk 2)
Working Cycle: 4 stroke
Disposition & number of cylinders: V 16
Bore and Stroke: 254 x 304.8 mm

Speed (maximum): 850 rpm
Piston–Swept Volume, total: 247 litres
Nominal Rating (to UIC 623): 2735 CV
Site Rating: 2620 CV
Turbocharged: Yes

TRANSMISSION

Type: Electric (d.c.)
Traction Generator: (1) English Electric Co. EE 840/6B
Traction Motors: (6) English Electric Co. EE 538/7A
Gear Ratio: 66:19

The general appearance should betray the origin of these British built locomotives! They were constructed on Merseyside at English Electric Co.'s. Vulcan Works, Newton le Willows, during 1968/69 and were, broadly based on British Rail's E.E. 'D400' (now Class 50) design. They constituted EE Traction division contract BAW 0005. The final details of which were formalized on June 7th 1968, though most design and some preparatory work had been completed by that date. The first unit, No. 1801, arrived by sea in Portugal on Boxing Day 1968, and entered traffic on January 13th 1969 - some six months ahead of schedule. All things considered, this was no mean feat! The last to be delivered, No. 1810, entered traffic on August 14th 1969.

Although the basic traction equipment corresponds with our Class 50, there the similarity ends. For instance, unlike their British counterparts, electronic equipment has not been used with the sole exception of the traction generator load regulator. All auxiliaries, excepting the two vacuum exhausters, have mechanical rather than electrical drives. Most engine, and many auxiliary, components are fully interchangeable with smaller EE '1401' class.

On account of the special interest which attaches to these British built locomotives some particulars of their English Electric traction equipment are summarized below.

Diesel Engine - This is of model 16CSVT Mk.II. As with class '1401', the reduced site rating of these machines (2584 bhp) is a direct consequence of conditions encountered in Portugal. In total, eleven engines were supplied for ten locomotives. These carry serial numbers IH 7320 - 7330. The same model of oil engine is installed in British Rail's Class 50 and in this application for a turbochargers are of Napier type HP 200/204. British Rail specified this layout because it provides a parts interchange facility with other EE engined locomotives and because it can be neatly accommodated within the British loading gauge. No such constraints existed in Portugal and advantage was taken of this to simplify the exhaust and charge air arrangements whereby the alternative layout was adopted. Only two large four entry turbochargers of Napier type HP 210/211 are deployed, one at each end of the engine. This exhaust system gives rise to a greater degree of gas excitation than in our Class 50 layout. Consequently the '1801's' feature a much more pronounced turbocharger whistle than their British counterpart.

Continuous full field ratings for the principle electrical machines are as follows -

Traction Generator - EE840/6B, twelve pole. 1710 kW, 1800 A, 950 V, at 850 rpm.

Auxiliary Generator - EE913/3A, four pole, belt driven. 30 kW, 273 A, 110 V over the speed range 1200 - 2270 rpm.

Traction Motors - EE538/7A, four pole. 338 hp, 600 A, 475 V at 526 rpm.

The '1801' class has an air/vacuum dual braking system. They can operate in multiple only with themselves or the '1401' class upto a total of two units. Other equipment installed includes 'Lubrovia' wheel flange lubricators.

Due to a derailment resulting in severe bogie damage, No. 1809 was withdrawn on 23rd June 1984, but its body shell has been retained as a spare, and during September 1989 was observed dumped at the rear of Barriero workshops in a rather sorry condition. It has since been removed to a compound behind the Barreiro roundhouse and its future now seems very uncertain.

These are the CP's fastest diesels, and originally performed the duties now undertaken by the Bombardier built '1961' class. They are now confined to the Southern Region, where seven of the nine surviving examples are diagrammed primarily on express passenger services. The main source of utilisation is on the services to the Algarve coast, covering all the Inter Regional and some Inter City turns. Prior to the problems with the '1901' class the '1801's' took charge of some heavy haul freight services off Barriero yard, including mineral trains serving the complex at Aljustrel. Fill in turns result in the class powering Barreiro - Setúbal locals, whilst from May 1990 a new IC service between Barreiro and Beja is booked for the type.

UIC Number Series 90-94-1-20

	Depot	Notes		Depot	Notes		Depot	Notes
1801-4	BAR		1805-5	BAR		1809-7	Wdn	1
1802-2	BAR		1806-3	BAR		1810-5	BAR	
1803-0	BAR		1807-1	BAR				
1804-8	BAR		1808-9	BAR				

1. Body stored behind Barreiro depot.

Introduced 1981

BUILDERS

Mechanical Parts: SOREFAME
Diesel Engine: S.A.C.M.
Transmission: Alsthom
Brakes: Knorr–Bremse

Builder's Type Code: AD 30 C
Deadman's System: Alsthom
Speed Recorder: 'HASLER'

DIMENSIONS

Height: 4310 mm
Width: 3062 mm
Bogie Pivot Centres: 9946 mm
Wheel Diameter (new): 1100 mm

Length over buffers: 19084 mm
Bogie Wheelbase: 4000 mm

PERFORMANCE

Maximum Speed: 100 km/h
Maximum Starting Tractive Effort: 39600 kg at **Factor of Adhesion:** (μ) 0.33

Tractive Effort at Continuous Rating: 25600 kg at 23.2 km/h
Tractive Effort at Maximum Speed: 6180 kg
Nominal Output at Rail: 2260 CV

WEIGHTS

Weight in Working Order: 117 tonnes
Adhesive Weight: 117 tonnes
Maximum Axleload: 19.9 tonnes
Diesel Engine: 12 tonnes
Traction Generator (Alternator): 3.8 tonnes
Traction Motor: 3.03 tonnes
Bogies, complete: 2 x 23.7 tonnes

SUPPLIES

Fuel Oil: 4.882 tonnes
Lubricating Oil: 0.5 tonnes
Coolant: 0.9 tonnes
Sand: 0.768 tonnes

DIESEL ENGINE

Number installed: 1
Builder: S.A.C.M.
Type: AGO V 12 DSHR
Working Cycle: 4 stroke
Disposition & number of cylinders: V 12
Bore and Stroke: 240 x 220/230 mm*

Speed (maximum): 1350 rpm
Piston–Swept Volume, total: 152.1 litres
Nominal Rating (to UIC 623): 3300 CV
Site Rating: 3000 CV
Turbocharged: Yes

* MGO/AGO diesel engines have articulated connecting rods, resulting in a different piston stroke for each cylinder bank.

TRANSMISSION

Type: Electric (a.c./d.c.)
Traction Alternator: (1) Alsthom AT 53
Traction Motors: (6) Alsthom TAO 659 (d.c.)
Gear Ratio: 69:17

These imposing, handsome (and rather noisy!) locomotives are very obviously French in appearance, incorporating the Paul Arzene style 'negative rake' frontend treatment which has become a hallmark, not only of S.N.C.F. traction, but also of so many French export designs.

These two ostensibly almost identical batches were constructed by SOREFAME under an Alsthom licence, the '1901' series being intended primarily for freight haulage and the '1931' series for mixed traffic duties. Two subvariations of the Alsthom TAO 659 traction motor design are therefore utilised - TAO 659 C1 and TAO 659 P.

The really interesting feature of this delivery batch is that the locomotives incorporate an Alsthom dynamic braking system, which provides a maximum braking effort at the wheel rim of 22500 kg at 42.5 km/h. In fact, these are the only CP diesels so fitted. Locomotives of this series are also visibly different from of the '1931'by virtue of their prominent protruding buffer stocks.

Equipment installed provided only for compressed air train braking. Multiple unit operation is catered for; they can multiple with themselves upto a total of four units. Vogel wheel flange lubricators are fitted as standard.

These locomotives are quite sophisticated and most capable locomotives, but ones which have proved to be somewhat fragile in traffic. They are powered by S.A.C.M./AGO 'D' series articulated connecting rod engines, which were first introduced at 2735 CV UIC nominal rating during the late 1960's. Unlike these lower rated predecessors, and also unlike their older and very successful MGO relatives, this newer and highly rated version has proved troublesome. Serious component failures have occurred. The problems have not been totally resolved, despite the fact that these engines are site rated at less than their UIC nominal rating. Consequently, an effort has been made to diagram these units for duties involving the minimum possible engine load cycling. Furthermore, the engine support systems, notably the cooling arrangements, are sophisticated and prone to give rise to problems. The resolution of these engine problems will know doubt ultimately affect the long term pattern of deployment of other types of locomotive, such as the English Electric '1801' class.

They are all allocated to Barreiro depot, and provide the motive power for much of the freight operations centred on Barreiro yard. This freight traffic can take them as far afield as the yard at Vila Nova de Gaia, just south of Porto. As already mentioned, engine problems have brought a need for less arduous duties and from September 1987 these locomotives took over all the Barreiro - Faro Inter City (orginally termed 'Rapido') diagrams from the '1801's, though currently the motive power on these services is more diverse.

UIC Number Series 90-94-1-22

	Depot	Notes		Depot	Notes		Depot	Notes
1901-8	BAR		1906-7	BAR		1911-7	BAR	
1902-6	BAR		1907-5	BAR		1912-5	BAR	
1903-4	BAR		1908-3	BAR		1913-3	BAR	
1904-2	BAR		1909-1	BAR				
1905-9	BAR		1910-9	BAR				

▲ The rack-back windscreen makes the 1901 and 1931 Classes recognisable as of French origins. No. 1912 is dumped next to the mainline at Barreiro in September 1989. (David N.Clough)

Introduced 1981

BUILDERS

Mechanical Parts: SOREFAME
Diesel Engine: S.A.C.M.
Transmission: Alsthom–EFACEC
Brakes: Knorr–Bremse

Builder's Type Code: AD 30 C
Deadman's System: Alsthom
Speed Recorder: 'HASLER'

DIMENSIONS

Height: 4310 mm
Width: 3062 mm
Bogie Pivot Centres: 9946 mm

Wheel Diameter (new): 1100 mm
Length over buffers: 18756 mm
Bogie Wheelbase: 4000 mm

PERFORMANCE

Maximum Speed: 120 km/h
Maximum Starting Tractive Effort: 39600 kg at **Factor of Adhesion**: (μ) 0.33
Tractive Effort at Continuous Rating: 25600 kg at 23.2 km/h
Tractive Effort at Maximum Speed: 5280 kg
Nominal Output at Rail: 2260 CV

WEIGHTS

Weight in Working Order: 116.5 tonnes
Adhesive Weight: 116.5 tonnes
Maximum Axleload: 19.6 tonnes
Diesel Engine: 12 tonnes
Sand: 0.768 tonnes
Traction Generator (Alternator): 3.8 tonnes
Traction Motor: 3.03 tonnes
Bogies, complete: 2 x 23.7 tonnes

SUPPLIES

Fuel Oil: 4.882 tonnes
Lubricating Oil: 0.5 tonnes
Coolant: 0.9 tonnes

DIESEL ENGINE

Number installed: 1
Builder: S.A.C.M.
Type: AGO V 12 DSHR
Working Cycle: 4 stroke
Disposition & number of cylinders: V 12
Bore and Stroke: 240 x 220/230*mm

Speed (maximum): 1350 rpm
Piston–Swept Volume, total: 152.1 litres
Nominal Rating (to UIC 623): 3300 CV
Site Rating: 3000 CV
Turbocharged: Yes

* MGO/AGO diesel engines have articulated connecting rods, resulting in a different piston stroke for each cylinder bank.

TRANSMISSION

Type: Electric (a.c./d.c.)
Traction Alternator: (1) Alsthom AT 53
Traction Motors: (6) Alsthom TAO 659 (d.c.)
Gear Ratio: 69:17

This series was designed for mixed traffic duties and certain important differences exist between them and their slightly older cousins. Also, their main electrical machines were manufactured under Alsthom licence by the Portuguese concern EFACEC (Empresa Fabril de Maquinas Eléctricas S.A.).

The '1931' class locomotives (which entered traffic during 1981/82) does not incorporate a dynamic braking system. Furthermore the conventional braking arrangement has been changed to provide for dual/vacuum train braking. Other facilities are common but they, have a maximum speed than the '1901's (75 mph). Interestingly, they have been prepared to receive electric train supply equipment should it be deemed necessary to install this at some future date. Comments made in respect of the '1901' series apply equally here, but this mixed traffic design has also proved to be prone to bogie fires after periods of sustained heavy braking.

The class operates from Entroncamento depot and are freight duties take them quite far afield, including Barreiro, Setúbal, Lisboa and Vila Nova de Gaia. There are a few passenger diagrams from Entroncamento to the Spanish frontier, whilst Barreiro does sometimes make use of the class on Setúbal locals, but this latter utilisation may change from timetable to timetable.

A few remarks are pertinent regarding the cabs and controls of these Alsthom Atlantique locomotives in general. Their instrument desks are most interesting and unusual. The power controller is not the usual continental handwheel variety, but is actually a spring-loaded vertical 'joystick', where the power selected is decided, not by the angular degree of movement of the controller, but by the time it is held in the 'run-up' or 'run-down' positions (Compare the PBL braking controllers on, for example, our own Class 58 and Class 59 locomotives). On the '1901' series, a two position selector switch is incorporated, rendering the 'joystick' functional in either a traction or dynamic braking mode.

Curiously, a fixed cab seats are not provided, but rather a portable 'barstool' type arrangement is the order of the day. Both these latter features seem to be an Alsthom specialty, for they can also be found in the class '9601' metre gauge diesel multiple units.

UIC Number Series 90-94-1-22

	Depot	Notes		Depot	Notes		Depot	Notes
1931-5	ENT		1937-2	ENT		1943-0	ENT	
1932-3	ENT		1938-0	ENT		1944-8	ENT	
1933-1	ENT		1939-8	ENT		1945-5	ENT	
1934-9	ENT		1940-6	ENT		1946-3	ENT	
1935-6	ENT		1941-4	ENT		1947-1	ENT	
1936-4	ENT		1942-2	ENT				

▲ A pair of Entroncamento 1931 class locomotives No's 1939 and 1940 are stabled at Campolide depot on 22nd April 1990. *(Geoff Hurst)*

Introduced 1979
Works No's M6101.01-13

BUILDERS

Mechanical Parts: BOMBARDIER (ex MLW)
Diesel Engine: BOMBARDIER (ex MLW)
Transmission: General Electric (Canada)
Brakes: Knorr–Bremse

Builder's Type Code: MXS–627
Deadman's System: 'SIFA–DEUTA'
Speed Recorder: 'HASLER'

DIMENSIONS

Height: 4210 mm
Width: 3048 mm
Bogie Pivot Centres:
Wheel Diameter (new): 1016 mm

Wheel Diameter (new): 1016 mm
Length over buffers: 19895 mm
Bogie Wheelbase: 3404 mm

PERFORMANCE

Maximum Speed: 120 km/h
Maximum Starting Tractive Effort: 45000 kg at **Factor of Adhesion** (μ) 0.38
Tractor Effort at Continuous Rating: 28200 kg at 18.75 km/h
Tractive Effort at Maximum Speed: 5500 kg
Nominal Output at Rail: 2250/1950 CV

WEIGHTS

Weight, tare: 114.5 tonnes
Weight in Working Order: 121 tonnes
Adhesive Weight: 121 tonnes
Maximum Axleload: 20.3 tonnes
Diesel Engine: 19 tonnes
Traction Generator: 5.32 tonnes
Traction Motor: 3.16 tonnes
Bogies, complete: 2 x 25.28 tonnes

SUPPLIES

Fuel Oil: 3.4 tonnes
Lubricating Oil: 0.81 tonnes
Coolant: 1.5 tonnes
Sand: 0.6 tonnes

DIESEL ENGINE

Number installed: 1
Builder: BOMBARDIER (ex MLW)
Type: 251–E
Working Cycle: 4 stroke
Disposition & number of cylinders: V 16
Bore and Stroke: 228.6 x 266.7 mm

Speed (maximum): 1050 rpm
Piston–Swept Volume, total: 175 litres
Nominal Rating (to UIC 623): 3042 CV
Site Rating: 3042 CV
Turbocharged: Yes

TRANSMISSION

Type: Electric (a.c./d.c.)
Traction Alternator: (1) General Electric (Canada) GTA–17 PC 1
Traction Motors: (6) CGE – 785 PA 1
Gear Ratio: 81:22

ELECTRIC TRAIN SUPPLY

AEG 1500V 50 Hz 420 kVA 443 CV

Montreal Locomotive Works was operated by MLW–Worthington until 1975, when it was sold to Bombardier, Inc. Since that date, the latter has been one of the three leading North American locomotive builders, being a major Canadian enterprise.

The '1961' series was constructed at Montreal by Bombardier's Rail & Diesel Products Division, under Sales Order No. 4736. The model type is designated CCF - MXS 627. Despite their Canadian origins, these are not truly typical North American units. They are a special twin–cab export design, featuring a full width body.

These are CP's 'really powerful diesels' (but only marginally so) and, regrettably, not one of their most stylish. However this is the only diesel class to be equipped for electric train supply. They have dual train braking installation, and can operate in multiple with themselves up to a total of four units. Vogel wheel–flange lubricators are fitted as standard.

No. 1961 itself was written–off, (together with SOREFAME/English Electric 'steeple cab' No. 1439), in Sud Express disaster, on the Beira Alta line. The remaining twelve operate on the Northern Region, and are allocated to the depot at Figueira da Foz. They are equally at home on passenger or freight services, and can be observed to advantage at Pampilhosa, where they are seen hauling trains 'under the wires' over the main north-south electrified route, or at Sta. Comba Dão line.

They were introduced to provide an electric train supply capability for hauling services such as the international workings to Paris (nowadays feature S.N.C.F. 'Corail' stock). Following their introduction in 1979 they displaced the English Electric '1801' class from these duties. Nowadays they spend much of their time hauling these services between Pampilhosa and Vilar Formoso. However, freight work does involve forays along the Porto - Lisboa main line as far south as Setil.

UIC Number Series 90-94-1-22

	Depot	Notes		Depot	Notes		Depot	Notes
1961-8	Wdn		1966-1	FIG		1971-1	FIG	
1962-0	FIG		1967-9	FIG		1972-9	FIG	
1963-8	FIG		1968-7	FIG		1973-7	FIG	
1964-6	FIG		1969-5	FIG				
1965-3	FIG		1970-3	FIG				

▲ The 1961 Class is unlikely to win an award for its looks but is equally at home on passenger or freight work. No. 1962 pauses at Coimbra-B on 3rd May 1990, with a van train from the Beira-Alta line bound for Barreiro. (David N.Clough)

2. BROAD GAUGE ELECTRIC LOCOMOTIVES

2501–2515   Bo-Bo

Introduced 1956–57

BUILDERS

Mechanical Parts: (50 Hz Groupement) Alsthom–Henschel
Electrical Traction Equipment: Alsthom/Siemens/Jeumont–Schneider
Transmission: Alsthom
Brakes: Freins Jourdain–Monneret   **Deadman's System:** 'OERLIKON'
Builder's Type Code: Bo–Bo–2500   **Speed Recorder:** 'HASLER'

DIMENSIONS

Height (pantograph retracted): 4450 mm   **Bogie Pivot Centres:** 7500 mm
Width: 3105 mm   **Bogie Wheelbase:** 3200 mm
Length over Buffers: 15380 mm   **Wheel Diameter (new):** 1300 mm

PERFORMANCE

Maximum Speed: 120 km/h
Maximum Starting Tractive Effort: 19500 kg at **Factor of Adhesion:** (μ) 0.27
Tractor Effort at One–hour Rating: 13100 kg at 60.5 km/h
Tractive Effort at Continuous Rating: 12150 kg at 62 km/h
Tractive Effort at Maximum Speed: 4500 kg
Nominal Output at Rail: 2790 CV (2053 kW)

WEIGHTS

Weight, tare: 69.6 tonnes
Weight in Working Order: 72 tonnes
Adhesive Weight: 72 tonnes
Maximum Axleload: 18 tonnes
Transformer: 7.8 tonnes
Traction Motor: 3.2 tonnes
Bogies, complete: 2 x 16 tonnes

SUPPLIES

Transformer Oil: 1.52 tonnes
Sand: 0.66 tonnes

ELECTRICAL TRACTION EQUIPMENT

Transformer (Maker & Rating): Alsthom, 4365 kVA (25 kV)
Tap Changer (Maker & Type): Brown–Boveri, 22 step
Silicon Rectifier (Maker): Jeumont–Schneider
Silicon Rectifier (Configuration): Diodes in "Push–Pull"
Silicon Rectifier (Maximum Starting Current): 3000 A

TRANSMISSION

Traction Motors, Maker: Alsthom
Traction Motors, Type: (4) TAO– 645 A1
Traction Motors, One–hour Rating: 4 x 557 kW=2228 kW
Traction Motors, Continuous: 4 x 529 kW =2116 kW
Traction Motors, Characteristics: Fully–suspended, Force ventilated
Gear Ratio: 78:21

The '2501' series was built by the '50 Hz Groupement', and displaying a fair blend of contemporary styling practices. These were CP's first electric locomotives. As is universal in all four of the existing a.c. locomotive types, control is by high tension tap changer. As originally built, the '2501's' were equipped with water cooled ignitron rectifiers.

They are carried on Henschel bogies and have a dual (air/vacuum) train braking braking system. They have no dynamic braking equipment. Indeed, none of CP's electric locomotives have a dynamic brake despite the fact that rheostatic brakes are almost universally installed in the electric multiple unit fleet. There is also no multiple-unit facility and no provision for electric train supply. 'Lubrovia' wheel flange lubricators are fitted as standard.

In excess of thirty years old, they still perform invaluable work, which even now still includes some passenger duties. However their life expectancy has been substantially diminished, since tenders have now been invited for fourtythree new electric locomotives of 5600 kW (7510 hp) rating. Fourteen of which will be required for the forthcoming new electrification of the Pampilhosa - Vilar Formoso route, and the remainder for Lisboa - Porto services, permitting the phasing out of life expired stock.

UIC Number Series 90-94-0-27

	Depot	Notes		Depot	Notes		Depot	Notes
2501-6	ENT		2506-5	ENT		2511-5	ENT	
2502-4	ENT		2507-3	ENT		2512-3	ENT	
2503-2	ENT		2508-1	ENT		2513-1	ENT	
2504-0	ENT		2509-9	ENT		2514-9	ENT	
2505-7	ENT		2510-7	ENT		2515-6	ENT	

▲ The 0725 Lisboa Santa Apolónia to Guarda *Inter-Regional* train hauled by 2501 class No.2510 stands in Coimbra-B station on 3rd May 1990. *David N.Clough)*

2551–2570   **Bo-Bo**

Introduced 1963–64

BUILDERS

Mechanical Parts: (50 Hz Groupement) SOREFAME–Henschel
Electrical Traction Equipment: Alsthom/Siemens/Jeumont–Schneider
Transmission: Alsthom   **Builder's Type Code:** Bo–Bo–2500
Brakes: Freins Jourdain–Monneret   **Deadman's System:** 'OERLIKON'
Built under Licence from: Budd–Henschel   **Speed Recorder:** 'HASLER'

DIMENSIONS

Height (pantograph retracted): 4450 mm   **Bogie Pivot Centres:** 7500 mm
Width: 3003 mm   **Bogie Wheelbase:** 3200 mm
Length over Buffers: 15380 mm   **Wheel Diameter (new):** 1300 mm

PERFORMANCE

Maximum Speed: 120 km/h
Maximum Starting Tractive Effort: 18900 kg
Factor of Adhesion (μ) 0.27
Tractive Effort at One–hour Rating: 13100 kg at 58 km/h
Tractive Effort at Continuous Rating: 12150 kg at 60 km/h
Tractive Effort at Maximum Speed: 4500 kg
Nominal Output at Rail: 2790 CV (2053 kW)

WEIGHTS

Weight, tare: 68.1 tonnes
Transformer Oil: 1.52 tonnes
Weight in Working Order: 70.52 tonnes
Adhesive Weight: 70.52 tonnes
Maximum Axleload: 17.63 tonnes
Transformer: 7.8 tonnes
Traction Motor: 3.2 tonnes
Bogies, complete: 2 x 16 tonnes

SUPPLIES

Transformer Oil: 1.52 tonnes
Sand: 0.66 tonnes

ELECTRICAL TRACTION EQUIPMENT

Transformer (Maker & Rating): Alsthom, 4365 kVA (25 kV)
Tap Changer (Maker & Type): Brown–Boveri, 32 step
Silicon Rectifier (Maker): Jeumont–Schneider
Silicon Rectifier (Configuration): Diodes in 'Push–Pull'
Silicon Rectifier (Maximum Starting Current): 3000 A

TRANSMISSION

Traction Motors Maker: Alsthom
Traction Motors Type: (4) TAO– 645 A1
Traction Motors One–hour Rating: 4 x 557 kW 2228 kW
Traction Motors Continuous: 4 x 529 kW 2116 kW
Traction Motors Chacteristics: Fully–suspended, Force ventilated
Gear Ratio: 78:21

SOREFAME was established in 1943 at Amadora. In 1952, being aware of Portugal's growing need for railway material, the company set up a railway engineering department and by 1971, the plant and offices covered some eighteen acres. In 1953, a licensing agreement was signed with the Budd company of Red Lion Plant, Philadelphia, Pennsylvania, USA . This authorising SOREFAME to build stainless steel railway vehicles in Portugal. Manufacture started in 1955. Since then, construction of rolling stock with stainless steel bodywork has become a SOREFAME specialty. In the '2551' class they have extended this practice and as licence holders, have produced these most striking locomotives with *fluted* stainless steel body shells - No. 2551 was, in fact, the first electric locomotive in the world to be constructed in this material. The bodies are self supporting structures which provide a weight saving of some three tonnes over the early series. Aesthetically they were intended to harmonize with the contemporary stainless steel coaching stock by the same builder.

When delivered, the specifications of the electrical equipment were similar to that of the '2501' series. These too carried on Henschel bogies.

These locomotives are equipped with a dual (air/vacuum) train braking system. Almost surprisingly, as in the case with the other electric locomotives, they have no dynamic brake. There is also no provision for multiple working. 'Lubrovia' wheel flange lubricators are fitted as standard.

No's 2554 and 2555 were withdrawn some years ago. In 1986, No. 2567 was noted to be in a wrecked condition at Entrocamento, but has since been repaired and returned to traffic. To contain repair costs, a new body of the '2501' class pattern was constructed at Entroncamento Works. This latter establishment has been very resourceful indeed, for it does not have the capability to produce replacement stainless steel bodies of the correct pattern. No. 2558 was observed with severe accident damage in September of the same year but in this case sufficient funding has been made available to enable an almost totally rebuilt stainless steel body to be supplied by SOREFAME. This had been delivered to Entroncamento by May 1990. After fitting out, it should enable this locomotive to return to traffic in the not too distant future.

These locomotives can be observed on the electrified routes which emanate from Lisboa's Santa Apoló nia terminus to Porto Campanhã and beyond to Erminsinde. Alongside the 2501's, they haul both passenger and freight services. As regards the former workings, they are normally found on the Inter City diagrams nowadays. Since they have no electric train supply capability for the modern rolling stock. Their passenger duties include some of those which change traction at Entroncamento or Pampilhosa before proceeding onto non electrified lines.

As already mentioned, plans for new investment are anticipated to see these early types withdrawn in a few years time.

UIC Number Series 90-94-0-27

	Depot	Notes		Depot	Notes		Depot	Notes
2551-1	ENT		2558-6	ENT		2565-1	ENT	
2552-9	ENT		2559-4	ENT		2566-9	ENT	
2553-7	ENT		2560-2	ENT		2567-7	ENT	
2554-5	Wdn		2561-0	ENT		2568-5	ENT	
2555-2	Wdn		2562-8	ENT		2569-3	ENT	
2556-0	ENT		2563-6	ENT		2570-1	ENT	
2557-8	ENT		2564-4	ENT				

(**Front Cover**) English Electric 1801 Class No. 1803 (with temporary Temeraire nameplate) having arrived at Vila Real de Sto. António (Guadiana) with the overnight train from Barreiro in September 1989. *(David N.Clough)*

(**Rear Cover**) 2551 Class Stainless steel body electric awaits its next duty on Entroncamento depot, in September 1989. *(David N.Clough)*

▲ Although built with stainless steel bodies to match the coaches, the 2551 Class now spend the majority of their time on freight. No 2565 pauses at Pampilhosa on 3rd May 1990, with a mixed goods bound for Porto. *(David N.Clough)*

▼ Alsthom 2601 class electrics No's 2606 (on 1845 IR to Lisboa) and 2605 (on 1710 Rapido to Lisboa) stand at Porto Campanhã on 24th April 1990. *(Geoff Hurst)*

2601–2612   Bo-Bo

Introduced 1974

BUILDERS

Mechanical Parts: (50 Hz Groupement) Alsthom   **Builder's Type Code:** CP 6
Electrical Traction Equipment: Alsthom–BBC–TE–JS
Deadman's System: 'DAVIES & METCALFE'
Transmission: Alsthom   **Speed Recorder:** 'HASLER'
Brakes: WABCO (Westinghouse)

DIMENSIONS

Height (pantograph retracted): 4300 mm   **Bogie Pivot Centres:** 10294 mm
Width: 3057 mm
Bogie Wheelbase: 2200 mm
Length over Buffers: 17500 mm
Wheel Diameter (new): 1140 mm

PERFORMANCE

Maximum Speed: High Gear 160 km/h (Low Gear 100 km/h)
Maximum Starting Tractive Effort: High Gear 21000 kg (Low Gear 25000 kg)
Factor of Adhesion: (μ) High Gear 0.27 (Low Gear 0.32)
Tractive Effort at One–hour Rating: High Gear 12300 kg (Low Gear 19500 kg)
Tractive Effort at Maximum Speed: High Gear 6800 kg at 89 km/h (Low Gear 10080 kg at 55 km/h)
Tractive Effort at Continuous Rating: High Gear 11900 kg at 89 km/h (Low Gear 19150 kg at 55 km/h)
Nominal Output at Rail: 3900 CV (2870 kW)

WEIGHTS

Weight, tare: 75.4 tonnes
Weight in Working Order: 78 tonnes
Adhesive Weight: 78 tonnes
Maximum Axleload: 19.5 tonnes
Transformer: 6.4 tonnes
Traction Motor: 5.3 tonnes
Bogies, complete: 2 x 18.8 tonnes
Total, Mechanical Parts: 49 tonnes
Total, Electrical Parts: 28 tonnes

SUPPLIES

Transformer Oil: 1.6 tonnes
Sand: 0.6 tonnes

ELECTRICAL TRACTION EQUIPMENT

Transformer (Maker & Rating): Alsthom, 4150 kVA (25 kV)
Tap Changer (Maker & Type): Brown–Boveri 32 step
Silicon Rectifier (Maker): MTE/JS
Silicon Rectifier (Configuration): Diodes in Gräetz bridge formation
Silicon Rectifier (Maximum Starting Current): 1600 A

TRANSMISSION

Traction Motors, Maker: Alsthom
Traction Motors, Type: (2) TAB–660 A1
Traction Motors, One–hour Rating: 2 x 1500 kW 3000 kW
Traction Motors, Continuous: 2 x 1470 kW 2940 kW
Traction Motors, Chacteristics: Fully suspended, force ventilated. Monomotor bogies with bi–reduction ratio facility
Gear Ratios: High Gear 1.88:1 (Low Gear 2.87:1)

ELECTRICAL TRAIN SUPPLY

Maker: Alsthom, 1150 V A.C. 50Hz **Normal Rating:** 300 kVA
Pre–supply: 420 kVA

Another design unmistakably 'à la française'. The 'negative rake' frontend treatment was first introduced with the French National Railways (S.N.C.F.) CC-40100 series of four voltage units, and resulted from an engineer's decision to incline the driving cab windows inwards from the top. This is claimed to eliminate glare and reflection, and to provide the driver with a high degree of visibility in widely varying conditions. The actual original translation of this engineering decision into a design artform was the creation of S.N.C.F's house stylist, Paul Arzens. It gives these CP locos a modern and imposing appearance and in the authors' view are rather sleek and handsome. The body styling of this class was based on that of the SNCF BB-15000 series and the nose has been designed to protect the crew and locomotive equipment in the event of a level crossing impact or the like. (The CP mainlines abound with level crossings!)

These multi purpose locomotives were also supplied to the CP by the 50 Hz Groupement, with the French company MTE (Compagnie Matériel et Traction Electrique) acting as project manager. An original order for five units was later increased to twelve. These machines had silicon rectifiers from new and design of the class follows closely that of the fifteen Class E40 units supplied by the group in 1971 to Turkish State Railways (TCDD), which in turn were derived from SNCF BB-17000 series.

Mechanically and electrically they are also very much French in concept, for they have monomotor bogies with a bi-reduction gear ratio facility - a practice much cherished by French traction engineers. These bogies were specially developed for the Portuguese broad gauge and incorporate alternative gear ratios for 100 or 160 km/h (62 or 100 mph), according to traffic requirements. Actually the CP line speeds were restricted to 100 km/h until 1979, when these locomotives began working limited express services between Lisboa and Porto at upto 140 km/h (87 mph). Despite the monomotor arrangement the two ripple current type TAB 660 traction motors compare with motors of the earlier series, in as much as they are suspended with Alsthom flexible drive. These locomotives incorporate a Westinghouse (WABCO) PBL2 (Poussoir Bouton Locomotive) dual (air/ vacuum) train braking system, but again no dynamic brake and no multiple unit facility either. 'Lubrovia' flange lubricators are installed.

The Class 2621 are the CP's newest and most powerful electric locomotives. Generally they represent a repeat order for '2601' type locomotives, but this time construction was in Portugal by SOREFAME, under licence. Differences do exist and largely concern the control of the braking system. On the '2601' series the vacuum exhauster operates continuously, irrespective of the braking requirements of the train being hauled. This is because the locomotives' braking control system requires a vacuum, whereas on the newer locomotives the exhauster only runs when the vacuum braked trains are actually being worked.

In view of their very recent introduction, it is surprising that they do not incorporate thyristor control of traction motor voltage, though this has been applied experimentally to a few electric multiple units. Again there is no dynamic brake.

Unlike the older classes of electric locomotive, the '2601's' boast electric train supply. Together with the newer '2621' series, they are the mainstay of the Lisboa (Santa Apolónia) – Porto Inter–City services and Inter Regional services. However, they do take a hand in some freight operations.

UIC Number Series 90-94-0-38

	Depot	Notes		Depot	Notes		Depot	Notes
2601-1	CAP		2605-2	CAP		2609-4	CAP	
2602-9	CAP		2606-0	CAP		2610-2	CAP	
2603-7	CAP		2607-8	CAP		2611-0	CAP	
2604-5	CAP		2608-6	CAP		2612-8	CAP	

UIC Number Series 90-94-0-39

	Depot	Notes		Depot	Notes		Depot	Notes
2621-7	CAP		2624-1	CAP		2627-4	CAP	
2622-5	CAP		2625-8	CAP		2628-2	CAP	
2623-3	CAP		2626-6	CAP		2629-0	CAP	

3. METRE GAUGE LOCOMOTIVES

9001–9003/9004–9006*   Bo-Bo

Introduced CP 1975 (Built ◇1958 ★ 1964 ∗ 1965 + 1967)

BUILDERS

Mechanical Parts: Alsthom
Diesel Engine: S.A.C.M.
Transmission: Alsthom
Brakes: Freins Jourdain–Monneret

Builder's Type Code: BB 48T (BB 44T*)
Deadman's System: 'Hollande'
Speed Recorder: 'Teloc'

DIMENSIONS

Height: 3700 mm
Width: 2550 mm
Length over buffers: 11174 mm

Bogie Pivot Centres: 5850 mm
Bogie Wheelbase: 2200 mm
Wheel Diameter (new): 950 mm

PERFORMANCE

Maximum Speed: 70 km/h
Maximum Starting Tractive Effort: 11500 kg
Factor of Adhesion: (μ) 0.25
Tractive Effort at Continuous Rating: 11000 kg at 15 km/h
Tractive Effort at Maximum Speed: 2400 kg
Nominal Output at Rail: 625 CV

WEIGHTS

Weight in Working Order: 46 (43*) tonnes
Adhesive Weight: 46 tonnes
Maximum Axleload: 11.5 tonnes
Diesel Engine: 4.3 tonnes
Traction Generator: 2.84 tonnes
Traction Motor: 1.32 tonnes

SUPPLIES

Fuel Oil: 1.67 tonnes
Lubricating Oil: 0.133 tonnes
Coolant: 0.365 tonnes
Sand: 0.54 tonnes

DIESEL ENGINE

Number installed: 1
Builder: S.A.C.M.
Type: MGO V 12 ASHR
Working Cycle: 4 stroke
Disposition & number of cylinders: V 12

Bore and Stroke: 175 x 180/192 mm
Speed (maximum): 1500 rpm
Piston–Swept Volume, total: 54 litres
Nominal Rating (to UIC 623): 925 CV
Site Rating: 850 (775*) CV

TRANSMISSION

Traction Generator (dc): (1) Alsthom 830 H 10
Traction Motors: (4) Alsthom TA 641 M
Gear Ratio: 79.14

UIC Number Series 90-94-1-06

	Depot	Located	Ex.		Depot	Located	Ex.
9001-2◇	BOA	Boa Vista	FT1022	9004-6★	BOA	Boa Vista	FT1025
9002-0∗	BOA	Livraçao	FT1023	9005-3★	BOA	Sernada	FT1026
9003-8∗	BOA	Boa Vista	FT1024	9006-1+	BOA	Mirandela	FT1027

9021–9031

Introduced 1976/1978*

BUILDERS

Mechanical Parts: Alsthom
Diesel Engine: S.A.C.M.
Transmission: Alsthom
Brakes: Comp. des Freins Westinghouse

Builder's Type Code: AD 12 B
Deadman's System: 'Vacma'
Speed Recorder: 'HASLER'

DIMENSIONS

Height:
Width: 2800 mm
Length over buffers: 11360 mm

Bogie Pivot Centres: 5850 mm
Bogie Wheelbase: 2200 mm
Wheel Diameter (new): 950 mm

PERFORMANCE

Maximum Speed: 70 km/h
Maximum Starting Tractive Effort: 11500 kg
Factor of Adhesion: (μ) 0.25
Tractive Effort at Continuous Rating: 10600 kg at 21.5 km/h
Tractive Effort at Maximum Speed: 2150 kg
Nominal Output at Rail: 830 CV

WEIGHTS

Weight, tare: 43 tonnes
Weight in Working Order: 46.8 tonnes
Adhesive Weight: 46.8 tonnes
Maximum Axleload: 11.7 tonnes
Diesel Engine: 4.3 tonnes
Traction Generator: 2.84 tonnes
Traction Motor: 1.32 tonnes

SUPPLIES

Fuel Oil: 2.52 tonnes
Lubricating Oil: 0.133 tonnes
Coolant: 0.4 tonnes
Sand: 0.54 tonnes

DIESEL ENGINE

Number installed: 1
Builder: S.A.C.M.
Type: MGO V 12 ASHR
Working Cycle: 4 stroke
Disposition & number of cylinders: V 12

Bore and Stroke: 175 x 180/192 [†] mm
Speed (maximum): 1500 rpm
Piston–Swept Volume, total: 54 litres
Nominal Rating (to UIC 623): 1050 CV
Site Rating: 1000 CV

TRANSMISSION

Traction Generator (dc): (1) Alsthom 830 H 10
Traction Motors: (4) Alsthom TA 641 M
Gear Ratio: 79.14

[†] MGO/AGO diesel engines have articulated connecting rods, resulting in a different piston stroke for each cylinder bank.

UIC Number Series 90-94-1-07

	Depot	Located		Depot	Located
9021-8	BOA	Mirandela	9027-5*	BOA	Régua
9022-6	BOA	Boa Vista	9028-3*	BOA	Mirandela
9023-4	BOA	Régua	9029-1*	BOA	Mirandela
9024-2	BOA	Boa Vista	9030-9*	BOA	Mirandela
9025-9	BOA	Mirandela	9031-7*	BOA	Mirandela
9026-7	BOA	Mirandela			

Both these types are closely related, and in fact, have the appearance somewhat reminiscent of our own British Rail English Electric Type 1 (Class 20) locomotives.

A prominent visual feature of all CP's metre gauge diesel locomotives is the presence of a solitary buffer located above each coupling. Locomotives 9001-9006 were purchased second hand from Ferrocarrill del Tajuña SA (FC), Madrid, Spain.

Locomotives 9001-9006 were built over a period of nine years, 9006 was built under Alsthom license by Euskalduna/GE Española. All others were built by Alsthom, 9004/5 were built at Belfort and the rest were constructed at Tarbes.

All types can operate in multiple with themselves. The early batch 9001-9006 series can multiple up to two locomotives, whilst the 9021-9031 series can multiple upto three engines. Only the latter class has wheel flange lubricators, which are of the 'Lubrovia type'.

The metre gauge diesels are divided between the surviving lines. The number to be found on each of the (isolated) sections varies according to need, but the majority are to be found working passenger services from Porto (Trindade) station (off Boa Vista depot), and from Tua in the Douro Valley to Bragança (off the sub shed at Mirandela). Other lesser centres of activity at Livração, and Régua (junction for Vila Real), both on the Douro Valley line, and Sernada do Vouga for the Vale do Vouga lines.

The different types appear to be used indiscriminantly, and also seem to be moved around the metre gauge network. This is presumably related to maintenance requirements, since maintenance is carried out at Boa Vista (next to Avenida da França station). Apart from use on freight (which appear as is minimal) some passenger services do appear to be loco hauled (see below). However, utilisation does vary on the Bragança line due to availability of the 9701 dmu's.

▲ 9004 stands at Trofa and awaits its return with 1945 Porto Trindade peak service consisting of three 1931 built coaches, on 24th April 1990. *(Geoff Hurst)*

4. BROAD GAUGE DIESEL UNITS

The codes used for diesel and electric multiple units are as used by British Rail and are as follows -

B-Brake C-Composite (First and Second Class) D-Driving F- First Class M-Motor S-Second Class T- Trailer

0051-0056 Series

Builder: NOHAB
Entered Service: 1947-48
Engine: Scania Vabis
Transmission: Hydraulic Lysholm-Smith
Wheel Arrangement: 1A-A1
Max.Speed: 80 kph (50 mph)

H.P.: 2 x 137/1 x 137*
Wheel diameter: 700 mm
Weight: 20.36/18* tonnes
Length over buffers: 1556 mm
Seating: 8F 32S
Former Number: M^Y51-56

The C.P. ordered from Nyquist & Holm (AB NOHAB) of Trollhätten, Sweden six, four wheeled railcars. Three of which were twin engined and originally numbered X1101-03, whilst the other three were single engined and originally numbered X1151-53*. These railcars were of light-weight construction. The sequence renumbering is not known.

They worked various branchlines in the south of Portugal. They were out of service by 1981, however some were in existence in December 1989, but had disappeared by April 1990.

DMBC	Depot	Notes	DMBC	Depot	Notes	DMBC	Depot	Notes
7-020051-2	Wdn		7-020053-8	Wdn		7-020055-3	Wdn	
7-020052-0	Wdn		7-020054-6	Wdn		7-020056-1	Wdn	

0101-0115 Series

Builder: NOHAB
Entered Service: 1948
Engine: Scania Vabis
Transmission: Hydraulic Lysholm-Smith
Wheel Arrangement: 1A-A1
Max.Speed: 100 kph (62.5 mph)

H.P.: 2 x 137
Wheel diameter: 700 mm
Weight: DMBC 28 tonnes
Length over buffers: 2249 mm
Seating: DMBC 16F 56S TS 58S/TC 16F 38S
Former Number: M^Y101-115 R^Y101-111

The eleven Class 0101 bogie railcars, were at first numbered X101-106 and X1001-1005, and had two 137 bhp engines.

All NOHAB cars have the same model of diesel engine, by AB Scania Vabis of Södertälje, Sweden. It is an eight cylinder machine of 11.3 litres capacity and set to deliver 137 bhp at 1750 rpm. In all cars, the transmission is of Lysholm-Smith hydro-mechanical type. In broad gauge railcars each engine drives one axle.

The class 0101 railcars and non driving trailers are used to provide passenger services for the branch lines of Eastern Portugal. They were used on branches radiating from the mainlines :- Beja - Moura; Évora - Estramoz - Vila Viçosa; Portalegre - Estramoz and Setil - Vendas Novas, however all but the last line lost its passenger services on 1st January 1990. They now work on locals and cross border duties from Portalegre to Badajoz (Spain). A single railcar is also based at Tunes for an early morning service from Santa Clara-Sabóla to Tunes. The trailers are still in limited use.

DMBC	Depot	Notes	DMBC	Depot	Notes	DMBC	Depot	Notes
7-020101-5	BAR		7-020106-4	BAR		7-020111-4	BAR	
7-020102-3	Wdn		7-020107-2	BAR		7-020112-2	BAR	
7-020103-1	Wdn		7-020108-0	BAR		7-020113-0	BAR	
7-020104-9	Wdn		7-020109-8	BAR		7-020114-8	BAR	
7-020105-6	BAR		7-020110-6	BAR		7-020115-5	BAR	

Trailer Cars

TS/TC*	Depot	Notes	TS/TC*	Depot	Notes	TS/TC*	Depot	Notes
37-29101-5	BAR		37-29105-7	Wdn		37-29109-8	Wdn	
37-29102-3*	BAR		37-29106-4	Wdn		37-29110-6	Wdn	
37-29103-1*	BAR		37-29107-2	Wdn		37-29111-4*	BAR	
37-29104-9	BAR		37-29108-0*	BAR				

0301-0325 Series

Builder: ALLAN
Entered Service: 1954
Engine: AEC
Transmission: Electric
Wheel Arrangement: Bo-Bo
Max.Speed: 100 kph (62.5 mph)

H.P.: 360
Wheel diameter: 920mm
Weight: DMBC 51.5/TS 31.5 tonnes
Length over buffers: 2233 mm
Seating: DMBC 24F 50S/TS 106S
Former Number: M^{Y}301-325 R^{Y}301-312

N.V.Allan of Rotterdam, Netherlands delivered in 1954-55 a broad gauge railcar, and is four metres (13ft) shorter than its NS version. It is of all steel construction. The brake is vacuum (Jourdain Monneret) and the vacuum cylinders are carried on the bogies. Air brake equipment and pneumatic control is by Knorr. Rheostatic braking is included on each railcar, with resistance grids mounted at each end of the railcar.

Each railcar has two floor mounted 11.3 litre AEC engines, pressure charged by a Buchi-Brown turboblower set, with a top output of 200 bhp at 1800 rpm.

These Allan railcars and non driving trailers work the branch lines of Central Portugal. The trailers were used as locomotive hauled stock for a time in the 1980s. All railcars are based at Coimbra B, and be found working local coastal services from Cacem to Caldas da Rainha, Figueira da Foz and Alfarelos, Coimbra Parque to Serpins, Coimbra - Figueira da Foz via Pampilhosa services. One railcar is based at Guarda for local services to Vilar Formoso. The use of trailers appears to have ceased and pairs of railcars are common. Railcars are stabled at Campolide Diesel depot (Lisboa) as well as Figueria da Foz and Coimbra. A few trailers can be found at Figueira da Foz (in a very poor state) and one at Barriero!

DMBC	Depot	Notes	DMBC	Depot	Notes	DMBC	Depot	Notes
8-030301-7	COI		8-030310-8	COI		8-030319-9	COI	
8-030302-5	COI		8-030311-6	Wdn		8-030320-7	COI	
8-030303-3	COI		8-030312-4	COI		8-030321-5	COI	
8-030304-1	COI		8-030313-2	COI		8-030322-3	COI	
8-030305-8	COI		8-030314-0	COI		8-030323-1	COI	
8-030306-6	COI		8-030315-7	COI		8-030324-9	COI	
8-030307-4	COI		8-030316-5	COI		8-030325-6	COI	
8-030308-2	COI		8-030317-3	COI				
8-030309-0	Wdn		8-030318-1	COI				

Trailer Coaches

TS	Depot	Notes	TS	Depot	Notes	TS	Depot	Notes
22-29301-8	COI		22-29305-9	COI	1	22-29309-1	Wdn	
22-29302-6	Wdn		22-29306-7	COI		22-29310-2	COI	
22-29303-4	COI	1	22-29307-5	COI		22-29311-0	Wdn	
22-29304-2	COI	1	22-29308-3	COI		22-29312-8	COI	

1. Derelict at Figueira da Foz

◄ Rebuilt Coimbra Parque station sees the arrival of a pair of 0301 railcars 0301 and 0312 with the 1707 from Serpins. *(Geoff Hurst)*

0401-0419

Builder: SOREFAME
Entered Service: 1965/66*
Engine: Rolls Royce
Transmission: Hydraulic Rolls Royce
Wheel Arrangement: 1A A1 + 2' 2'
Max.Speed: 110 kph (68.75 mph)
H.P.: 2 x 348

Max. Traction Effort: 6200 kg
Wheel diameter: 850 mm
Weight: 94.1 tonnes
Length over buffers: 5196 mm
Seating: 105S
Former Number: $M^{YFC}401\text{-}19\ R^{YFC}401\text{-}19$

These stainless steel bodied diesel multiple units can be found in northern Portugal on lines radiating from Porto. They work local passenger trains down the Douro Valley as far as Tua, Porto to Braga, Viana do Castelo, Valença and Monçao (this branch was closed on 1st January 1990). The Porto - Vigo (España) service is booked for these units. They can multiple with 0601 units.

DMS	DTBC	Depot	Notes	DMS	DTBC	Depot	Notes
7-050401-2	5-000401-7	CAM		7-050411-1	5-000411-6	CAM	
7-050402-0	5-000402-5	CAM		7-050412-9	5-000412-4	CAM	
7-050403-8	5-000403-3	CAM		7-050413-7	5-000413-2	CAM	
7-050404-6	5-000404-1	CAM		7-050414-5	5-000414-0	CAM	
7-050405-3	5-000405-8	CAM		7-050415-2*	5-000415-7*	CAM	
7-050406-1	5-000406-6	CAM		7-050416-0*	5-000416-5*	CAM	
7-050407-9	5-000407-4	CAM		7-050417-8*	5-000417-3*	CAM	
7-050408-7	5-000408-2	CAM		7-050418-6*	5-000418-1*	CAM	
7-050409-5	5-000409-0	CAM		7-050419-4*	5-000419-9*	CAM	
7-050410-3	5-000410-8	CAM					

► 0401 dmu DTBC No.0417 awaits its next duty at Porto Campanhã station on 1st May 1990. *(David N.Clough)*

0501-0506 Series

Builder: Fiat
Entered Service: 1953
Engine: OM
Transmission: Mechanical Fiat
Wheel Arrangement: 2B + B2
Max.Speed: 120 kph (75 mph)
Former Number: $M^Y501\text{-}506\ R^Y501\text{-}506\ M^Y501\text{-}506$

H.P.: 480
Wheel diameter: 910 mm
Weight: 56.5 tonnes
Length over buffers: 27780 mm
Seating: DMBF 64F TRBF 46F

In 1953 an order was placed with Fiat for a luxury triple multiple unit for the fast service between Lisboa and Porto, entering service in the Summer of 1953, completing the journey in four and a half hours.

The main feature was the long frame of 26670 mm (87ft 6ins), it had air conditioning (the equipment housed in the roof), a kitchen and space for luggage and mail. It seated 174 first class passengers. The engines were located in the driving cars and were O.M.-Saurer 12 cylinder twin bank horizontal engine of type SBD, with a top output of 505 bhp at 1400 rpm and drove a Fiat five speed gearbox.

Electrification of the mainline in 1966 caused these units to be transfered to the Southern area, where they worked the *'Sotavento'* expresses until withdrawal in 1981. Some cars have been converted to departmental use as breakdown vans.

DMBF	Depot	Notes
6-030501-4	Wdn	Dumped at Entroncamento
6-030502-2	Wdn	
6-030503-0	Wdn	Preserved at Estremoz

DMBF	Depot	Notes
6-030504-8	BAR	BDV 80-94-975-0002-9
6-030505-5	Wdn	Dumped at Torre da Gadanha
6-030506-3	BAR	BDV 80-94-975-0003-7

TRBF	Depot	Notes
5-990501-5	Wdn	BDV at Barreiro ???
5-990502-3	Wdn	Dumped at Entroncamento

TRBF	Depot	Notes
5-990503-1	Wdn	Dumped at Torre da Gadanha

0601-0640/0651-0662*Series

Builder: SOREFAME
Entered Service: 1979/1989*(TS 1989-90)
Engine: SFAC
Transmission: Hydraulic Voith
Wheel Arrangement: 2'B-B'2
Max.Speed: 120 kph (75 mph)

H.P.: 383
Wheel diameter: 920 mm
Weight:
Length over buffers: 5348 mm
Seating: DMBC 40F/38S DMS/TS 116S

Originally built as two car diesel multiple units they perform the same duties in Northern Portugal as the 0401 units, being found more on the Douro Valley line. Twenty six trailers were ordered (some to be used with 0651 units) to make them into three car units. A number of units have a green strip painted along the windows and the name *Inter-Citides* added. These units normally work the *Rapido* services from Porto to Viana do Castelo and Régua.

The 0651 sets are purpose built as three car units in 1989-90. They are based at Figueira da Foz and are to be found on Lisboa Rossio - Caldas da Rainha *Inter-Regionals* and *Rapidos* services, they also work local passenger services. Trailers are still being delivered and these can be found in any set, some 0601 trailers have been viewed in 0651 sets!

DMBC	TS	DMS	Depot	Notes
7-030601-2	5-990601-4*	7-030621-0	CAM	
7-030602-0	5-990602-2*	7-030622-8	CAM	
7-030603-8	5-990603-0*	7-030623-6	CAM	
7-030604-6	5-990604-8*	7-030624-4	CAM	
7-030605-3	5-990605-5*	7-030625-1	CAM	
7-030606-1	5-990606-3*	7-030626-9	CAM	
7-030607-9	5-990607-1*	7-030627-7	CAM	
7-030608-7	5-990608-9*	7-030628-5	CAM	
7-030609-5	5-990609-7*	7-030629-3	CAM	
7-030610-3	5-990610-5*	7-030630-1	CAM	
7-030611-1	5-990611-3*	7-030631-9	CAM	
7-030612-9	5-990612-1*	7-030632-7	CAM	
7-030613-7	5-990613-9*	7-030633-5	CAM	
7-030614-5	5-990614-7*	7-030634-3	CAM	
7-030615-2	5-990615-4*	7-030635-0	CAM	
7-030616-0	5-990616-2*	7-030636-8	CAM	
7-030617-8	5-990617-0*	7-030637-6	CAM	
7-030618-6	5-990618-8*	7-030638-4	CAM	
7-030619-4	5-990619-6*	7-030639-2	CAM	
7-030620-2	5-990620-4*	7-030640-0	CAM	
7-030651-7*	5-990621-2*	7-030657-4*	FIG	
7-030652-5*	5-990622-0*	7-030658-2*	FIG	
7-030653-3*	5-990623-8*	7-030659-0*	FIG	
7-030654-1*	5-990624-6*	7-030660-8*	FIG	
7-030655-8*	5-990625-3*	7-030661-6*	FIG	
7-030656-6*	5-990626-1*	7-030662-4*	FIG	

▲ 0601 Class dmu No.0602, with Rolls Royce engines, waits at Tua, after arriving from Porto, before returning down the Douro Valley, in September 1990. *(David N.Clough)*

0751-0766 Series

Builders: Macosa/CAF/CAF-MMC/Verdingen
Entered Service: 1968 (Purchased from RENFE 1979-80)
Engine: SFAC
Transmission: Mechanical Pegaso-Z1
Wheel Arrangement: AA - 11
Max.Speed: 90 kph (56 mph)

H.P.: 277
Wheel diameter: 900 mm
Weight: DMS 32/DTS 30.5 tonnes
Length over buffers:
Seating: DMS 46S DTS 60S

The CP purchased sixteen secondhand class 591 four wheeled, two car multiple units from RENFE in 1979/80. The sequence of renumbering is not known. The power cars and some trailers FRCs were built by Macosa, CAF, and CAF-MMC, with some trailers (FRCs) being built by Astilleros de Cadiz, Euskalduna and Verdingen.

These units appear to have been a failure, with some sets being out of use by 1981. By 1985 only three sets remained in stock. Today only one set has been retained for use as a staff train for Entroncamento depot.

DMBS	DTS	Depot	Notes	DMBS	DTS	Depot	Notes
6-020751-9	5-000751-7	Wdn		6-020759-2	5-000759-8	Wdn	
6-020752-7	5-000752-5	Wdn		6-020760-0	5-000760-6	Wdn	
6-020753-5	5-000753-1	Wdn		6-020761-8	5-000761-4	Wdn	1
6-020754-3	5-000754-9	Wdn		6-020762-6	5-000762-2	Wdn	1
6-020755-0	5-000755-6	Wdn		6-020763-4	5-000763-0	ENT	2
6-020756-8	5-000756-4	Wdn	1	6-020764-2	5-000764-8	Wdn	
6-020757-6	5-000757-2	Wdn	1	6-020765-9	5-000765-5	Wdn	
6-020758-4	5-000758-0	Wdn		6-020766-7	5-000766-3	Wdn	3

1. Dumped at Entroncamento 2. **Staff train** 3. **Dumped at Pamphilhosa**

▶ Derelict railcar 0766 was found on Pampilhosa depot on 25th April 1990. *(Geoff Hurst)*

5. METRE GAUGE DIESEL UNITS

9001-9008 Series

Builder: CP Lisboa
Entered Service: 1948
Engine: Chevrolet
Transmission: Mechanical
Wheel Arrangement: 1A
Seating: 11F 16S/7F 21S*

Max.Speed: 60 km/h (38 mph)
H.P.: 90
Wheel diameter: ? mm
Weight: ? tonnes
Length over buffers: ? mm
Former Number: ME1-ME6/ME7-ME8*

These railcars ended their days working the *Támega* Livraçao to Arco da Bauhle and the *Sabor* Pocinho to Miranda do Douro branch lines. They were all out of use by December 1981.

DMBC	Depot	Notes	DMBC	Depot	Notes	DMBC	Depot	Notes
6-019001-2	Wdn		6-019004-6	Wdn		6-019007-9	Wdn	2
6-019002-0	Wdn		6-019005-3	Wdn		6-019008-7	Wdn	
6-019003-8	Wdn	1	6-019006-1	Wdn				

1. Preserved as M3 at Arco de Baulhe 2. Preserved as M6 at Lousado

9051-9054/9055* Series

Builder: Val do Vouga Sernada
Entered Service: 1941-4/1947*
Engine: Chevrolet
Transmission: Mechanical
Wheel Arrangement: 2A
Seating: 10F 15S

Max.Speed: 60 km/h (38 mph)
H.P.: 90/93*
Wheel diameter: ? mm
Weight: ? tonnes
Length over buffers: ? mm
Former Number: ME51-ME54/ME55*

The Val do Vouga (VV) Railway - built railcars remained on these lines until their withdrawal. They were all out of service by December 1981.

DMBC	Depot	Notes	DMBC	Depot	Notes	DMBC	Depot	Notes
6-019051-7	Wdn	1	6-019053-3	Wdn	1	6-019055-8*	Wdn	
6-019052-5	Wdn		6-019054-1	Wdn				

1. Preserved in Macinhata do Vouga Museum

9101-9103 Series

Builder: NOHAB
Entered Service: 1949
Engine: Scania Vabis
Transmission: Hydraulic Lysholm-Smith
Wheel Arrangement: B-B
Seating: 8F 28S

Max.Speed: 70 km/h (43 mph)
H.P.: 2 x 137
Wheel diameter: 700 mm
Weight: 22 tonnes
Length over buffers: 15500 mm
Former Number: ME^{Y}101 - ME^{Y}103

The CP placed an order for three metre gauge railcars; they were originally numbered XE1001-1003. Because of the steep gradients each railcar is twin engined, each driving an axle.

The Támega line from Livraçao to Arco da Baule was a mixture of locomotive hauled trains and NOHAB railcars, however since the demise of the passenger service beyond Amarante. One railcar is sufficent to operate the service. The other two are usually stabled at Livraçao.

DMBC	Depot	Notes	DMBC	Depot	Notes	DMBC	Depot	Notes
7-029101-6	LIV		7-029102-4	LIV		7-029103-2	LIV	

► NOHAB railcar 9101 awaits to depart Livraçao with the 1225 to Amarante on 23rd April 1990. *(Geoff Hurst)*

9301-9310 Series

Builder: ALLAN
Entered Service: 1954
Engine: AEC
Transmission: Electric Smith
Wheel Arrangement: Bo-Bo
Seating: 12F 32S

Max.Speed: 70 km/h (43 mph)
H.P.: 2 x 160
Wheel diameter: 820 mm
Weight: DMBC 36.64 (TS 20.36) tonnes
Length over buffers: 19510 mm
Former Number: ME^{Y}301 - ME^{Y}310 RE ^{Y}301-308

N.V. Allan of Rotterdam supplied in 1954 to the CP, ten railcars and ten trailers. The bodies are all steel. To suit existing stock the metre gauge railcars are fitted with Knorr straight air brakes, but with vacuum braking for the trailers. Rheostatic braking is also incorporated in the railcars, with the resistance grids carried on the roof at each end.

This class used to work the north Porto system as well as the Corgo valley line from Régua to Chaves. Today they are based on the Vale do Vouga system at Sernada. Due to withdrawal of passenger services from Santa Comba Dão to Viseu and Sernada to Viseu on 1st January 1990, plenty of railcars can be found at the depot at Sernada. The use of trailers appears to be concentrated on the Espinho to Sernada section whilst pairs of railcars are common on the Aveiro to Sernada line.

DMBC	Depot	Notes	DMBC	Depot	Notes	DMBC	Depot	Notes
8-039301-8	SER		8-039305-9	SER		8-039309-1	Wdn	
8-039302-6	Wdn		8-039306-7	SER		8-039310-9	SER	
8-039303-4	SER		8-039307-5	SER				
8-039304-2	Wdn		8-039308-3	SER				

Trailer Cars

TS	Depot	Notes	TS	Depot	Notes	TS	Depot	Notes
28-29301-4	SER		28-29304-8	SER		28-29307-1	SER	
28-29302-2	SER		28-29305-5	SER		28-29308-9	??	
28-29303-0	SER		28-29306-3	SER				

► Two Allan railcars stand at Sernada on 25th April 1990. The railcar on the left is 9306 (just arrived from Aveiro) and on the right 9305 (is about to depart to Espinho). *(Geoff Hurst)*

9601-9622 Series

Builder: Alsthom
Entered Service: 1976/7
Engine: SFAC
Transmission: Electric Alsthom
Seating: DMS 52S DTBC 18F 24S

Max.Speed: 90 km/h (56 mph)
H.P.: 383
Wheel diameter: 880 mm
Weight: 64.36 tonnes

The 9601 units were purpose built two car units for the Porto metre gauge system, either working in single sets or pairs for the peak periods. Due to capacity problems at peak periods these units cannot provide all the trains for the service and two trains in each peak are locomotive hauled stock.

DMS	DTBC	Depot	Notes	DMS	DTBC	Depot	Notes
8-039601-1	5-009601-3	BOA		8-039612-8	5-009612-0	BOA	
8-039602-9	5-009602-1	BOA		8-039613-6	5-009613-8	BOA	
8-039603-7	5-009603-9	BOA		8-039614-4	5-009614-6	BOA	
8-039604-5	5-009604-7	BOA		8-039615-1	5-009615-3	BOA	
8-039605-2	5-009605-4	BOA		8-039616-9	5-009616-1	BOA	
8-039606-0	5-009606-2	BOA		8-039617-7	5-009617-9	BOA	
8-039607-8	5-009607-0	BOA		8-039618-5	5-009618-7	BOA	
8-039608-6	5-009608-8	BOA		8-039619-3	5-009619-5	BOA	
8-039609-4	5-009609-6	BOA		8-039620-1	5-009620-3	BOA	
8-039610-2	5-009610-4	BOA		8-039621-9	5-009621-1	BOA	
8-039611-0	5-009611-2	BOA		8-039622-7	5-009622-9	BOA	

◄ Porto Trindade is host to Alsthom Class 9601 units on 1st May 1990. *(David N.Clough)*

9701-9720 Series

Builder: Djuro Djaković
Entered Service: 1966-68 (CP 1980)
Engine: Fiat
Transmission: Mechanical Fiat
Wheel Arrangement: 2'B - B'2
Seating: DMS 36S MBC 18F 20S
Ex- Jugoslav Railways (JZ): DMS B802.001-20 MBC B802.501-20

Max.Speed: 60 km/h (38 mph)
H.P.: 185
Wheel diameter: 750 mm
Weight: 23 tonnes
Length over buffers: ? mm

These attractive little diesel multiple units were purchased second hand in 1980 from Jugoslav Railways (JZ). All were originally 760 mm gauge, and were converted to metre gauge operation, before entering service on the CP in 1981-82. The sequence of renumbering by the CP is not known. Car Nos. 9721-9740 are intermediate motor coaches and have no driving cabs. All cars have a 2B axle layout, each has one Fiat 185 hp diesel engine with mechanical transmission driving onto the two axles at one end only.

It was intended to operate these as four car sets in formations of DMS+MBC+MBC+DMS, however these units have proved very troublesome, with large numbers dumped out of use. These cars are split up between depots at Mirandela and Régua, whilst at Sernada do Vouga, some cars are stored inside and others are semi derelict off their bogies.

The Régua to Vila Real line are formed of two car sets, whilst the Tua to Bragança line has three car sets.Some of which have repainted in the modified CP livery and refurbished internally

DMS	Depot	Notes	DMS	Depot	Notes	DMS	Depot	Notes
6-019701-7	MIR		6-019708-2 r	MIR		6-019715-7	MIR	
6-019702-5	REG		6-019709-0 r	MIR		6-019716-5	MIR	
6-019703-3	REG		6-019710-8 r	MIR		6-019717-3	REG	
6-019704-1	Wdn		6-019711-6 r	MIR		6-019718-1	REG	
6-019705-8	REG		6-019712-4 r	MIR		6-019719-9	REG	
6-019706-6	??		6-019713-2	REG				
6-019707-4 r	MIR		6-019714-0	REG				

MBC	Depot	Notes	MBC	Depot	Notes	MBC	Depot	Notes
6-019720-7	??		6-019727-2	MIR		6-019734-8		1.
6-019721-5	MIR		6-019728-0	MIR		6-019735-5		1.
6-019722-3 r	MIR		6-019729-8	MIR		6-019736-3 r	MIR	
6-019723-1		1.	6-019730-6 r	MIR		6-019737-1	MIR	2.
6-019724-9		1.	6-019731-4		2.	6-019738-9	MIR	
6-019725-6		1.	6-019732-2	MIR		6-019739-7	??	
6-019726-4	??		6-019733-0		2.	6-019740-5	st	3.

r refurbished
1. Sernada Derelict 2. Out of Use 3. Sernada do Vouga

▶ Refurbished 9701 class units 9707 + 9730 + 9710 are stabled outside Mirandela depot on 23rd April 1990. Note the different CP livery . *(Geoff Hurst)*

6. BROAD GAUGE ELECTRIC UNITS

The first 25 kV AC electric multiple units delivered to the CP were the 2001-25 series. They are built by SOREFAME using the Budd patent stainless steel body. The electrical equipment was supplied by the 50 Hz Groupement composed of AEG, Siemens, LHB, Brown Boveri, Schinduer, Alsthom, SFAC, and Sorefame.

All of the 2001 2051 and 2082 units are based at Campolide depot and work the intensive local service on the Sintra, Cintura and onto the Lisboa to Entroncamento mainline as far as Sacevém and Vila Franca de Xira.

The later build of electrical units in the 2101 and 2151 series are Budd patent stainless steel and are based at Entroncamento. They have higher rated traction motors to operate the faster mainline services. They can be found on locals along the mainline from Lisboa Santa Apolónia to Entroncamento, Tomar, Coimbra, Aveiro, and Porto São Bento, as well as branch services from Coimbra to Figueira da Foz and Porto north to São Romão.

In February 1991, the CP placed an order with Siemens for 42 three car units to be delivered in Summer 1992 and to work the Sintra and Cintura lines. The 2001/2051 and 2082 units will be surplus and withdrawn.

2001-2025

Builder: SOREFAME
Electrical Equipment: 50 Hz Groupement
Wheel Arrangement: Bo-Bo + 2'2' + 2'2'
Max.Speed: 90km/h (56 mph)
Former No.: M^{YFC} 2001-25 R^{YFC} 2001-25 RP^{YFC} 2001-25
Seating: DMS/DTS 88S TBF 68F
Entered Service: 1956
Supply: 25kv 50hz AC Overhead
Wheel diameter: (Bo-Bo) 1000mm (2'2') 850mm
H.P.: 1469

DMS	TBF	DTS	Depot
9-142001-6	5-992001-5	5-002001-3	CAP
9-142002-4	5-992002-3	5-002002-1	CAP
9-142003-2	5-992003-1	5-002003-9	CAP
9-142004-0	5-992004-9	5-002004-7	CAP
9-142005-7	5-992005-6	5-002005-5	CAP
9-142006-5	5-992006-4	5-002006-2	CAP
9-142007-3	5-992007-2	5-002007-0	CAP
9-142008-1	5-992008-0	5-002008-8	CAP
9-142009-9	5-992009-8	5-002009-6	Wdn
9-142010-7	5-992010-6	5-002010-4	CAP
9-142011-5	5-992011-4	5-002011-2	Wdn
9-142012-3	5-992012-2	5-002012-0	CAP
9-142013-1	5-992013-0	5-002013-8	CAP
9-142014-9	5-992014-8	5-002014-6	CAP
9-142015-6	5-992015-5	5-002015-3	CAP
9-142016-4	5-992016-3	5-002016-1	Wdn
9-142017-2	5-992017-1	5-002017-9	CAP
9-142018-0	5-992018-9	5-002018-7	CAP
9-142019-8	5-992019-7	5-002019-5	CAP
9-142020-6	5-992020-5	5-002020-3	CAP
9-142021-4	5-992021-3	5-002021-1	CAP
9-142022-2	5-992022-1	5-002022-9	CAP
9-142023-0	5-992023-9	5-002023-7	CAP
9-142024-8	5-992024-7	5-002024-5	Wdn
9-142025-5	5-992025-4	5-002025-2	CAP

2051-2074/2082-2090*

Builder: SOREFAME
Electrical Equipment: 50 Hz Groupement
Wheel Arrangement: Bo-Bo + 2'2' + 2'2'
Max.Speed: 90 km/h (56 mph)
Weight: DTS 31.5 tonnes
Former No.s: M^{YFC}2051-74/81-90 R^{YFC}2051-74/81-90 RP^{YFC} 2051-74/81-90
Seating: DTS 88S MBC 56F 42S
Entered Service: 1962/1966*
Supply: 25kv 50hz AC Overhead
Wheel diameter: (Bo-Bo) 1000mm (2'2') 850mm
H.P.: 1469
Length: DTS 1682 mm

DTS	MBC	DTS	Depot	Notes
9-142051-3	5-992051-2	5-002051-0	CAP	
9-142051-1	5-992051-0	5-002051-8	CAP	
9-142052-9	5-992052-8	5-002052-6	CAP	
9-142053-7	5-992053-6	5-002053-4	CAP	
9-142054-5	5-992054-4	5-002054-2	CAP	
9-142055-3	5-992055-2	5-002055-0	CAP	
9-142056-0	5-992056-9	5-002056-7	CAP	
9-142057-8	5-992057-7	5-002057-5	CAP	
9-142058-6	5-992058-5	5-002058-3	CAP	
9-142059-4	5-992059-3	5-002059-1	CAP	
9-142060-2	5-992060-1	5-002060-9	CAP	
9-142061-0	5-992061-9	5-002061-3	CAP	
9-142062-8	5-992062-7	5-002062-9	CAP	
9-142063-6	5-992063-5	5-002063-7	CAP	
9-142064-4	5-992064-3	5-002064-5	CAP	
9-142065-1	5-992065-0	5-002065-8	CAP	
9-142066-9	5-992066-8	5-002066-6	CAP	
9-142067-7	5-992067-6	5-002067-4	CAP	
9-142068-5	5-992068-4	5-002068-2	CAP	
9-142069-3	5-992069-2	5-002069-0	CAP	
9-142070-1	5-992070-0	5-002070-8	CAP	
9-142071-9	5-992071-8	5-002071-6	CAP	
9-142072-7	5-992072-6	5-002072-4	CAP	
9-142073-5	5-992073-4	5-002073-2	CAP	
9-142074-3	5-992074-2	5-002074-0	CAP	
9-142082-6	5-992082-5	5-002082-3	CAP	
9-142083-4	5-992083-3	5-002083-1	CAP	
9-142084-2	5-992084-1	5-002084-9	CAP	
9-142085-9	5-992085-8	5-002085-6	CAP	
9-142086-7	5-992086-6	5-002086-4	CAP	
9-142087-5	5-992087-4	5-002087-2	CAP	
9-142088-3	5-992088-2	5-002088-0	CAP	
9-142089-1	5-992089-0	5-002089-8	CAP	
9-142090-9	5-992090-8	5-002090-6	CAP	

▲ Lisboa Rossio terminus is host three Sintra line electric units No.s 2044; 2003 and 2064 on 22nd April 1990. *(Geoff Hurst)*

2101-2124

Builder: SOREFAME
Entered Service: 1970
Electrical Equipment: 50 Hz Groupement
Supply: 25kv 50hz AC Overhead
Wheel Arrangement: Bo-Bo $+2'2' +2'2'$
Wheel diameter: (Bo-Bo) 1000mm (2'2') 850mm
Former No.s: M^{YFC}2101-24 R^{YFC}2101-24 RP^{YFC} 2101-24
Seating: DTS 71S MBF 60F DTS 88S

DTS	MBF	DTS	Depot
5-002101-1	9-172101-9	5-002102-9	ENT
5-002103-7	9-172102-7	5-002104-5	ENT
5-002105-2	9-172103-5	5-002106-0	ENT
5-002107-8	9-172104-3	5-002108-6	ENT
5-002109-4	9-172105-8	5-002110-2	ENT
5-002111-0	9-172106-6	5-002112-8	ENT
5-002113-6	9-172107-4	5-002114-4	ENT
5-002115-1	9-172108-2	5-002116-9	ENT
5-002117-7	9-172109-0	5-002118-5	ENT
5-002119-3	9-172110-8	5-002120-1	ENT
5-002121-9	9-172111-6	5-002122-7	ENT
5-002123-5	9-172112-4	5-002124-3	ENT
5-002125-0	9-172113-2	5-002126-8	ENT
5-002127-6	9-172114-0	5-002128-4	ENT
5-002129-2	9-172115-7	5-002130-0	ENT
5-002131-8	9-172116-5	5-002132-6	ENT
5-002133-4	9-172117-3	5-002134-2	ENT
5-002135-9	9-172118-1	5-002136-7	ENT
5-002137-5	9-172119-9	5-002138-3	ENT
5-002139-1	9-172120-7	5-002140-9	ENT
5-002141-7	9-172121-5	5-002142-5	ENT
5-002143-3	9-172122-3	5-002144-1	ENT
5-002145-8	9-172123-1	5-002146-6	ENT
5-002147-4	9-172124-9	5-002148-2	ENT

2151-2186/2201-2230*

Builder: SOREFAME
Entered Service: 1977/1984*
Electrical Equipment: Siemens-AEG-Oerlikon
Supply: 25kv 50hz AC Overhead
Wheel Arrangement: Bo-Bo $+2'2' +2'2'$
Wheel diameter: (Bo-Bo) 1000mm (2'2') 850mm
Max.Speed: 120 km/h (75 mph)
H.P.: 1716
Seating: DTS 96S MBF 60F

DTS	MBF	DTS	Depot
5-002151-6	9-172151-2	5-002152-4	ENT
5-002153-2	9-172152-0	5-002154-0	ENT
5-002155-7	9-172153-8	5-002156-5	ENT
5-002157-3	9-172154-6	5-002158-1	ENT
5-002159-9	9-172155-3	5-002160-7	ENT
5-002161-5	9-172156-1	5-002162-3	ENT
5-002163-1	9-172157-9	5-002164-9	ENT
5-002165-6	9-172158-7	5-002166-4	ENT
5-002167-2	9-172159-5	5-002168-0	ENT
5-002169-8	9-172160-3	5-002170-6	ENT
5-002171-4	9-172161-1	5-002172-2	ENT
5-002173-0	9-172162-9	5-002174-8	ENT
5-002175-5	9-172163-7	5-002176-3	ENT
5-002177-1	9-172164-5	5-002178-9	ENT
5-002179-7	9-172165-2	5-002180-5	ENT
5-002181-3	9-172166-0	5-002182-1	ENT
5-002183-9	9-172167-8	5-002184-7	ENT
5-002185-4	9-172168-6	5-002186-2	ENT
5-002201-9	9-172201-5	5-002202-7	ENT
5-002203-5	9-172202-3	5-002204-3	ENT

5-002205-0	9-172203-1	5-002206-8	ENT
5-002207-6	9-172204-9	5-002208-4	ENT
5-002209-2	9-172205-6	5-002210-0	ENT
5-002211-8	9-172206-4	5-002212-6	ENT
5-002213-4	9-172207-2	5-002214-2	ENT
5-002215-9	9-172208-0	5-002216-7	ENT
5-002217-5	9-172209-8	5-002218-3	ENT
5-002219-1	9-172210-6	5-002220-9	ENT
5-002221-7	9-172211-4	5-002222-5	ENT
5-002223-3	9-172212-2	5-002224-1	ENT
5-002225-8	9-172213-0	5-002226-6	ENT
5-002227-4	9-172214-8	5-002228-2	ENT
5-002229-0	9-172215-5	5-002230-8	ENT

▲ A 2151 series electric muiltiple unit (formed of 002156 172153 and 002155) is stabled in the northbay of Entroncamento staion on 22nd April 1990. *(Geoff Hurst)*

▼ Estoril line DC electric L301 works as pilot at Cais do Sodré depot on 4th May 1990. *(David N.Clough)*

7. ESTORIL

The Estoril Railway opened throughout, in 1895, from Lisboa (Cais do Sodré) along the coast to Cascais. It is 16 miles (26 km) long and is virtually isolated from the rest of the railway network in Portugal. This was the first railway in Portugal to be electrified. Sociade Estoril took over the line on a lease, with the provision it was electrified. In 1924 an order was placed with Allgemeine Elektrizitäts-Gesellschaft of Berlin (AEG) for electrification of the line, using 1500 V DC overhead lines. The locomotives were supplied by AEG, but the wooden bodied multiple units were built by two companies, Baume & Marpent of Morlanwelz suppling the power cars and Dyle & Bacalan of Bordeaux providing the trailers. Electrification was completed on 15th August 1926. The locomotives were used on freight and the "Sud Express" portion to Cascais. In 1948 an order was placed with General Electric Company (GEC) Great Britain Ltd for a larger locomotive, it was subcontracted to North British Locomotive Company of Glasgow . It was to be push compatible with pull the present units as well as the new Cravens units. The two AEG electrics were converted to push pull use. The North British locomotive was numbered 101 and had a brakevan/security area for conveying mails and valuables.

New stainless steel Budd design units were built by Sorefame in 1959-1961 and in 1970. Some cars use the frame of the original 1926 wooden bodied units. Sociade Estoril was nationalised in 1976 and passed to the CP. The numbering has not been altered to CP's UIC series. Another batch of stainless steel were delivered in 1979. Today upto seven cars operate the intensive service to Cascais, and the three platform stations at Oeiras and Sâo Pedro enabling locals to terminate and turn round without interferring with the intensive peak service.

The Units are based at Cais do Sodré depot next to the Lisboa terminus, and stable in the station precincts and at Cascais. The AEG locomotive is kept at Cascais and is painted in green with the Sociade Estoril logo on its side, it appears to be out of use. The North British locomotive is located at Cais do Sodré and works as depot pilot, and may be used to rescue failed units.

L301 — Bo-Bo

Builder: North British
Electrical Equipment: GEC (GB)
Weight: 51 tonnes

Entered Service: 1948
Wheel Diameter: 1016 mm (40 inches)
Max. Tractive Effort: 40000 lbs

	Depot	Notes
L301	CAS	Formerly 101

L302 — Bo-Bo

Builder: AEG
Entered Service: 1924 (Rebuilt SOREFAME 1950)

	Depot	Notes			Depot	Notes
L302	CAS	Located at Cascais		L303	Wdn	

101-111

Built: 1950
Builder: Cravens
Electrical Equipment: GEC (GB)

Supply: 1500V DC Overhead
Weight: ???
Seating: B^M 52S BA^C 54S

DTS	MS	DTS	Depot	DTS	MS	DTS	Depot
AB^C101	B^M101	BA^C101	CAS	AB^C107	B^M107	BA^C107	CAS
AB^C102	B^M102	BA^C102	CAS	AB^C108	B^M108	BA^C108	CAS
AB^C103	B^M103	BA^C103	CAS	AB^C109	B^M109	BA^C109	CAS
AB^C104	B^M104	BA^C104	CAS	AB^C110	B^M110	BA^C110	CAS
AB^C105	B^M105	BA^C105	CAS	AB^C111	B^M111	BA^C111	CAS
AB^C106	B^M106	BA^C106	CAS				

112-124

Built: 1959/1979 M
Builder: SOREFAME
Electrical Equipment: GEC (GB)

Supply: 1500V DC Overhead
Weight: M 48.6 tonnes/ C^1 28.4 tonnes
Seating: C^1/C^2 62S B^D/B^M 75S

DTS	MS	DTS	Depot	DTS	MS	DTS	Depot
$C^2$112	M112	$C^1$112	CAS	$C^2$119	M119	$C^1$119	CAS
$C^2$113	M113	$C^1$113	CAS	$C^2$120	M120	$C^1$120	CAS
$C^2$114	M114	$C^1$114	CAS	$C^2$121	M121	$C^1$121	CAS
$C^2$115	M115	$C^1$115	CAS	$C^2$122	M122	$C^1$122	CAS
$C^2$116	M116	$C^1$116	CAS	$C^2$123	M123	$C^1$123	CAS
$C^2$117	M117	$C^1$117	CAS	$C^2$124	M124	$C^1$124	CAS
$C^2$118	M118	$C^1$118	CAS				

201-214

Built: 1959/1970 AC^2/1979 AC
Builder: SOREFAME
Electrical Equipment: GEC (GB)

Supply: 1500V DC Overhead
Weight: ???
Seating: AC/AC^2 52S B^D/B^M 75S

DTS	TS	MS	DTS	Depot
$AC^2$201	B^D201	B^M201	$AC^1$201	CAS
$AC^2$202	B^D202	B^M202	$AC^1$202	CAS
$AC^2$203	B^D203	B^M203	$AC^1$203	CAS
$AC^2$204	B^D204	B^M204	$AC^1$204	CAS
$AC^2$205	B^D205	B^M205	$AC^1$205	CAS
$AC^2$206	B^D206	B^M206	$AC^1$206	CAS
$AC^2$207	B^D207	B^M207	$AC^1$207	CAS
$AC^2$208	B^D208	B^M208	$AC^1$208	CAS
$AC^2$209	B^D209	B^M209	$AC^1$209	CAS
$AC^2$210	B^D210	B^M210	$AC^1$210	CAS
$AC^2$211	B^D211	B^M211	$AC^1$211	CAS
$AC^2$212	B^D212	B^M212	$AC^1$212	CAS
$AC^2$213	B^D213	B^M213	$AC^1$213	CAS
$AC^2$214	B^D214	B^M214	$AC^1$214	CAS

215-222

Built: 1979
Builder: SOREFAME
Electrical Equipment: GEC (GB)

Supply: 1500V DC Overhead
Weight: ???
Seating:

DTS	TS	MS	DTS	Depot
$C^2$215	$C^1$215	M215	$C^2$215	CAS
$C^2$216	$C^1$216	M216	$C^2$216	CAS
$C^2$217	$C^1$217	M217	$C^2$217	CAS
$C^2$218	$C^1$218	M218	$C^2$218	CAS
$C^2$219	$C^1$219	M219	$C^2$219	CAS
$C^2$220	$C^1$220	M220	$C^2$220	CAS
$C^2$221	$C^1$221	M221	$C^2$221	CAS
$C^2$222	$C^1$222	M222	$C^2$222	CAS

▲ Craven built B^M110 is stabled in the middle road of Lisboa Cais do Sodré terminus. It appears to be receiving fitters attention. *(David Carter)*

8. TRACK MACHINES

Broad gauge track machines are allocated to four areas, Figueira da Foz (FIG) Entroncamento (ENT), Barriero (BAR) and Vila Real Sto. Antonio (VRA), plus 2 allocated to DOS. They are based at specific locations and are given below.

No.	Depot		No.	Depot
DG102	DOS		DG103	DOS

No.	Depot	Based at	No.	Depot	Based at
DP102	BAR	Pegões	DP114	ENT	Alferrarede
DP103	ENT	São Torcato	DP115	ENT	Marvao
DP104	BAR	Águas de Moura	DP116	ENT	Portalegre
DP106	ENT	Casa Branca	DP117	VRA	Funcheira
DP107	ENT	Crato	DP118	ENT	Covilhã
DP109	VRA	Amoreias-Odemira	DP119	FIG	Mortiagua
DP110	FIG	Vila Franca das Naves	DP121	VRA	Castro Verde
DP111	BAR	Casa Branca	DP122	FIG	Celorico da Beira
DP112	VRA	Messines-Alte	DP123	ENT	Entroncamento
DP113	FIG	Vilar Formoso			

No.	Depot	Based at	No.	Depot	Based at	No.	Depot	Based at
DP202	FIG	Amieira	DP214	FIG	Guarda	DP224	VRA	Beja
DP203	ENT	Estremoz	DP215	ENT	Vale Peso	DP225	BAR	Sant.Cacém
DP204	BAR	Grândola	DP216	BAR	Alcácer do Sal	DP226	FIG	Coimbra-B
DP205	BAR	P.Novo	DP217	ENT	Santa Euladia	DP227	ENT	Sta. Cita
DP206	FIG	S.M.Porto	DP218	ENT	Casa Branca	DP228	BAR	Évora
DP207	FIG	Cantanhede	DP219	ENT	Pte. Sôl	DP229	ENT	Ameixial
DP208	ENT	Belmonte	DP220	BAR	Évora	DP230	ENT	Fronteira
DP209	ENT	Belver	DP221	BAR	Évora	DP231	VRA	Tunes
DP211	VRA	Olhâo	DP222	VRA	Beja	DP232	VRA	Funcheira
DP213	FIG	Mangualde	DP223	FIG	D.Portos	DP235	VRA	Portimâo

9. STEAM LOCOMOTIVES

Regular use of steam traction on the CP ended on the 1970's but many locomotives still exist. The CP numbered its broad and metre gauge locomotives in seperate series and if the number commenced with 0 it was a tank engine. All metre gauge locomotives were prefixed by "E" denoting *estreita* (narrow). Most metre gauge locomotives were renumbered into the UIC series, however the E number was retained on sole bar. The old E number is used in this book. Some steam locomotives have been retained for charter trains.

Steam locomotives can be found at numerous locations in Portugal. The list below gives the last location sighted. Many locos are in store and they are occasionaly moved between sites as their status changes.

A Active D Dumped M Museum Pl Plinthed Pr Preserved   St Stored

BROAD GAUGE Locomotives

	Built	Wheel	Built by	Status	Location
1	1862*	2-2-2	Beyer Peacock	Pr	Santarem
9	1875	2-4-0	Beyer Peacock	Pl	Braga
23	1875	0-6-0	Beyer Peacock	A	Contumil
135	1881	0-6-0	Hartmann	Pl	Entroncamento
167	1889	0-6-0	SACM	D	Entroncamento
211	1924	4-6-0	Henschel	Pl	Pamphilhosa Beira Alta 61
238	1904	4-6-0	Borsig	St	Entroncamento
248	1905	4-6-0	Borsig	St	Contumil
262	1898	4-6-0	Fives Lille	Pr	Entroncamento CP School
282	1910	4-6-0	Henschel	D	Vila Nova de Gaia
294	1913	4-6-0	Henschel	D	Vila Nova de Gaia
357	1911	4-6-0	Henschel	Pr	Entroncamento CP School
501	1925	4-6-0	Henschel	Pr	?
553	1924	4-6-0	Henschel	Pr	Santarem
701	1912	2-8-0	Schwarzkopf	D	Vila Nova de Gaia
754	1913	2-8-0	Schwarzkopf	St	Entroncamento
801	1930	4-8-0	Henschel	Pr	Vilar Formoso
832	1947	4-8-0	MTM	Pr	Entroncamento
855	1945	2-8-2	Alco	Pr	Entroncamento
001	1881	0-4-0T	Hartmann	Pr	Estremoz
002	1881	0-4-0T	Hartmann	Pr	Nine
003	1890	0-4-0T	Cockerill	Pl	Entroncamento
004	1890	0-4-0T	Cockerill	Pr	Entroncamento CP School
005	1901	0-4-0T	Cockerill	Pr	Estremoz
012	1902	0-4-0T	Henschel	St	Entroncamento
013	1889	0-6-2T	Beyer Peacock	Pl	Faro
014	1889	0-6-2T	Beyer Peacock	A	Contumil
027	1891	0-6-2T	Beyer Peacock	Pr	Estremoz (Rebuilt 1924)
033	1890	2-6-2T	Beyer Peacock	Pl	Faro (Rebuilt 1925 from 016)
042	1907	2-6-2T	Cockerill	Pr	Entroncamento
070	1944	2-6-4T	Oficinas Gerais	Pr	Entroncamento
072	1916	2-6-4T	SLM	D	Vila Nova de Gaia
094	1929	2-6-4T	Henschel	Pl	Entroncamento
0184	1925	2-8-4T	Henschel	D	Contumil
0186	1925	2-8-4T	Henschel	Pr	Estremoz
0187	1925	2-8-4T	Henschel	Pr	Nine
0190	1925	2-8-4T	Henschel	D	Contumil
0201	1923	2-8-4T	Henschel	St	Casa Branca
02049	1854	2-2-2T	Fairburn	P	Braga

METRE GAUGE Locomotives

	Built	Wheels	Built by	Status	Location
E1	1922	0-4-0T	Henschel	Pl	Régua
E41	1904	0-6-0T	Hohenzollern	M	Chaves
E52	1889	0-6-0T	Kessler	M	Macinhata do Vouga Named *Viseu*
E54	1889	0-6-0T	Kessler	P	Darque
E55	1889	0-6-0T	Kessler	M	Bragança
E82	1886	2-6-0T	Kessler	M	Bragança
E86	1886	2-6-0T	Kessler	M	Macinhata do Vouga

E92	1910	2-6-0T	O&K	S	Espinho
E97	1910	2-6-0T	O&K	A	Sernada do Vouga
E101	1907	2-6-0T	Kessler	Pr	Lousado
E103	1907	2-6-0T	Kessler	M	Santarem
E111	1904	2-6-0T	Kessler	Pr	Macinhata do Vouga
E113	1907	2-6-0T	Kessler	M	Bragança
E114	1907	2-6-0T	Kessler	A	Mirandela
E121	1904	4-6-0T	Borsig	M	Macinhata do Vouga
E122	1908	4-6-0T	Borsig	Pl	Macinhata do Vouga as VV22
E123	1908	4-6-0T	Borsig	P	Macinhata do Vouga
E124	1908	4-6-0T	Borsig	Pl	Torredeita
E132	1924	2-8-2Ts	Henschel	P	Macinhata do Vouga
E143	1931	2-8-2T	Henschel	P	
E144	1931	2-8-2T	Henschel	P	Lousado as Norte 104
E151	1905	0-4-4-0T	Henschel	P	Lousado
E161	1905	0-4-4-0T	Henschel	M	Chaves
E162	1905	0-4-4-0T	Henschel	S	Livarção
E163	1905	0-4-4-0T	Henschel		??
E164	1905	0-4-4-0T	Henschel	D	Tua
E165	1908	0-4-4-0T	Henschel	S	Livraçao
E166	1908	0-4-4-0T	Henschel	D	Tua
E167	1908	0-4-4-0T	Henschel	M	Arco do Baule
E168	1908	0-4-4-0T	Henschel	D	Tua
E169	1908	0-4-4-0T	Henschel	Pr	Vila Real
E170	1908	0-4-4-0T	Henschel	D	
E181	1923	2-4-6-0T	Henschel	Pr	Campanhã Works
E201	1911	2-4-6-0T	Henschel	D	Régua
E202	1911	2-4-6-0T	Henschel	D	Régua
E203	1911	2-4-6-0T	Henschel	M	Chaves
E204	1911	2-4-6-0T	Henschel	D	Régua
E205	1913	2-4-6-0T	Henschel	D	Régua
E206	1913	2-4-6-0T	Henschel	D	Régua
E207	1923	2-4-6-0T	Henschel	St	Campanhã Works
E208	1923	2-4-6-0T	Henschel	D	Régua
E209	1923	2-4-6-0T	Henschel	D	Régua
E210	1923	2-4-6-0T	Henschel	D	Régua
E212	1923	2-4-6-0T	Henschel	D	Régua
E213	1923	2-4-6-0T	Henschel	D	Lousado
E214	1923	2-4-6-0T	Henschel	D	Régua
E215	1923	2-4-6-0T	Henschel	D	Régua
E216	1923	2-4-6-0T	Henschel	Pl	Entroncamento CP School
E217	1923	2-4-6-0T	Henschel	D	Régua

▲ E114 stands at Brunheda with a two coach special from Tua to Mirandela on 10th September 1986. *(John Scrace)*